JUNGLE ANGEL: BATAAN REMEMBERED

copyright 1988
Maxine Kaiser Russell
1350 Russell Road North
Brainerd, Minnesota 56401

Except for brief quotations in
reviews, no part of this book may
be reproduced in any form without
written permission of the copyright owner.

First printing 1988
printed in the United States of America

by Bang Printing Company
Brainerd, Minnesota 56401

ISBN #0-9617894-1-7

ACKNOWLEDGEMENTS: This story was composed with the help and thoughts of many people. With thanks to Lt.-Col. Hortense McKay's sister Mabel (Mrs. Lloyd P. Gilbert), Winona, MN and brother Wallace McKay, Edina, MN for their assistance. For valuable material, my thanks to Mrs. Jackie MacDonald, widow of Lee MacDonald, a survivor and hero of Bataan. Appreciation goes to dear friends, Leola Buchite, Paul and Betty Cibuzar and Marion Dimmick for their helpful input. With special thanks also for the assistance of members of the American Legion Post #255, Brainerd, the Brainerd Branch of AAUW (American Association of University Women) and the Crow Wing County Historical Society. Likewise with deep gratitude to Eunice and Carl E. Erickson (a Lt.-Col. US Army retired) for reading the manuscript, lending wise suggestions, and with special thanks to him for writing the Epilogue. Finally, I extend gratitude to Captain Paul L. Ashton, MD, author of **Bataan Diary,** for permission to use some of his pictures and statistics.

1

*To Honor
Those
Courageous Nurses
With Whom I
Served
During World War II
In the Jungles
of the Philippines*

CONTENTS

INTRODUCTION by Maxine K. Russell

PART I
THE MCKAY STORY   Pages

Destination: The Philippines 19
Bataan Jungle 30
The Valiant Men of the USS Spearfish 36
Australian Interlude 42
A Salute to Sydney 46
Sizzling-Hot New Guinea 50
The Heartbreak at Leyte 52
Old Glory Raised Again 55
Twenty-four Years of Service 59
The Carillon Bells Toll for Her 66

PART II
BATAAN REMEMBERED   Pages

The Heroic Men of the Bataan Death March 75
In the words of Three Veterans

EPILOGUE Carl E. Erickson 90

PHOTO ALBUM
List of 36 pictures including two maps. 102

The Story of

HORTENSE E. MCKAY

A US ARMY NURSE

Who Served in WWII

In the Jungles of Luzon

as told to

Maxine K. Russell

Introduction

A NEW FRIEND-PLAID AND HEATHER

I first met Hortense McKay about sixteen years ago. It was shortly after my husband Bob and I moved to this Brainerd area of sparkling lakes and woodlands. I can't remember the social event, but I do remember the person, a slim, gray-haired lady about sixty years of age, modest of manner, with a kind smile and yet a somewhat sedate bearing. Most significantly I recall that she was wearing a blue and green tartan plaid (a cocktail dress), which made me think of heather and the Highland fling.

One afternoon over a cup of tea, I had an opportunity to visit with her again. This time her brow was knit and serious. She had just finished giving a talk to members of the Brainerd Branch of AAUW (American Association of University Women). Her erudite topic was "Women in Finance." She seemed totally familiar with the subjects of money management, investments, taxes and other weighty "female" financial problems. From listening to her, I knew that she was deeply concerned about the national debt and how it would affect all of us. She sighed, "We may soon be the world's largest debtor nation." Here's one woman I thought who knows how to balance a check book, something our Congress doesn't do well. But the reason is obvious. She's a thrifty Scot.

Then I asked her, "Hortense, did you graduate in Business or Economics?" I wondered what gave her this wealth of business experience.

"Why, no," was her reply. "I'm a Lieutenant-Colonel retired in the US Army Nurse Corps. Money matters are my hobby."

In no way, without knowing more about her personal life, could I ever have guessed that *Nursing* had been her profession.

LITTLE WHITE PAPER CAPS

Hortense McKay was born at home on July 16, 1910 in a tranquil little farmhouse near Harmony in Amherst Township, Fillmore County, southeastern Minnesota. My husband Bob and I had driven through this area once on our way back from Iowa. The fields were flourishing with millions of acres of corn. We were hunting for traces of the old Dubuque Trail, but instead, (Ah, serendipity!), we came upon a small town called Harmony. It advertised tours through an underground limestone cave.

"Once in a while the farmer gets lucky," Bob said, "when he discovers a cave on his land and can charge admission."

I remember how we went down several hundred feet into an enormous cave that had a long river and beautiful waterfall.

I said, "I wonder how many hidden secrets like this one exist on the inside of the earth?"

When I asked Hortense about the caves, she said, "Whenever we children would run along the road to school, the ground under our feet seemed to have a strange hollow sound. We weren't surprised to learn later that a nearby farmer had lost some of his pigs which accidentally disappeared into the ground. My father sometimes brought us limestone fossils home from the field. It was a beautiful place for us children to play. We were surrounded by miles of wildflowers."

I exclaimed, happily, "I played with lots of flowers too as a child, dancing among the daffodils. My father owned greenhouses."

"But ours were wildflowers—billions of them! My sister Mabel and I danced and ran around in them too. We'd pick huge armfuls of Moccasin flowers, Jack-in-the-Pulpits and many others—lots of them we didn't know their names.

"I guess wildflowers weren't protected by law as they are today. Some species have almost vanished completely," I said.

Hortense continued, "On May Day, we'd make little paper baskets and fill them with tiny wild things like hepatica, Johnny-Jump-Ups, and wild strawberry blooms. Then, we'd take our May baskets to favorite neighbors...you know the kind who baked cookies." She smiled recalling how good they were. "We'd hang our baskets on their door knobs. Once we even hung one like a little prayer on the Presbyterian Church door. There were some McKays buried in the churchyard which was right next to the church. It was built on high ground overlooking streams and hills."

Just like a pretty postcard picture, I thought.

"One of those little streams ran right through our farmyard. To cool off a bit in the hot summer, I'd ride my little Shetland pony, Miss Myrtle, through the water. When she did what I asked, I always gave her a clover treat."

"Miss Myrtle must have been a lovely pony," I replied. "I never had a pony, but Bob did. He lived on a farm too as a child."

"Yes, I had a lovely childhood, so secure. However, just after World War I, when I was about ten years old, our whole family came down with influenza. My mother, (Lydia Hahn McKay of German descent) was a schoolteacher. She knew most of the neighboring families and visited them when they were sick."

"Your mom was a brave woman".

"Yes, she was, but eventually she came down with the flu too. In those years, everyone was terrified by it. Some folks were alive one day and dead the next."

"How did you manage with your mother sick?"

"Well, we took turns with the chores. Mabel and I made ourselves little white paper caps like nurses wore in pictures we'd seen. First, we helped care for Mother, then Dad, then our two younger brothers, Peter and George, and even Inga, our hired girl. Wallace wasn't born until later after we had moved to Brainerd. One after another, they all came down with the flu. Finally, Mabel and I were stricken too. I guess that's the first time I ever thought much about sickness."

"It was a terrible epidemic," I said, nodding my head.

"For a while after that, everybody and everything looked sick to me. My little pony, the wild birds in the trees, and the little frogs in the creek even. I imagined all of them had the flu and they depended on me to take care of them. Even the carved wooden lions on the old chair in our living room needed me to nurse them back to health. Now, for the first time, I began to think about becoming a nurse, not just playing that I was one."

I interrupted her. "In fact, you thought so much about it that you spent the rest of your life as a nurse, didn't you?"

"Yes, thirty years or more."

"Long enough to become a Lieutenant-Colonel in the Army Nurse Corps. For a woman, in those years, that was a big achievement."

Among the wildflowers on the family farm near Harmony, MN. Sister Mabel at left, and Hortense at right. Circa 1916.

Two little girls with bows in their hair, Hortense (standing) and her sister Mabel. Spring of 1918.

For the first time, I began to realize how much suffering and death my friend had seen, how much love and service she had given and how much endurance and courage she really had. I couldn't uncover the intriguing story of her life all in one day. It would have to wait until the next time I met her. So meanwhile, my enquiring Muse, let the bagpipes play!

FROM PROBIE TO WHITE CAP

In the scrutinizing process of delving into the private life of someone, especially a friend, I was prepared to do some"undersea diving" for facts, hopefully to surface with unusual findings. I was well aware that the most compelling details of any person's life must be searched out and recorded, otherwise, all would vanish away as waves against the sand.

Some months later at a luncheon meeting of the University of Minnesota Alumni Group in Brainerd, quite by coincidence, Bob and I were seated next to Hortense McKay. Until then, I had no idea that in the early thirties Hortense and I were students at one and the same time stalking about the Minneapolis campus. With a student population of over 12,000, small wonder we had never met. I was in the Arts College studying Speech and Theatre. Hortense was a half-mile away in the College of Nursing. Both of us were submerged in antithetical areas of study. Ahem!

As we were being served our $5.00 cheeseburgers, Bob asked, "Hortense, did you ever eat any of those big five cent hamburgers at the campus White Castle?"

She grinned. "Of course, everybody did. They were certainly good value."

Munching away as I talked, I said to her, "We probably ate at the same counter unbeknown to each other."

"Probably, or we might have rubbed elbows in the Administration Building queuing up to pay our fee statements. My tuition then in the School of Nursing was only about $30.00 per quarter, and besides, the University supplied us with uniforms and our board and room free. But, with books and all, sometimes it wasn't easy to scrape the money together for tuition."

Bob, the checkbook balancer of our family, replied, "It was just as difficult then as it is today for students to come up with the tuition."

Hortense agreed. "We had a heavy curriculum. I was

required to take Physiology, Bacteriology and Anatomy with real cadavers. There were a number of other prerequisite courses too. Did you know, Maxine, that the University School of Nursing was the first in the USA to require these additional pre-nursing courses worked into the college curriculum?"

"I always heard that a degree in Nursing from the University of Minnesota was considered to be one of the very best at that time," I said.

"We were all called "Probies" or nurses on probation. It was somewhat like a novice in a convent. In those years of female discrimination, there were no nurses around the University Hospital who were married, not even our Dean, Katherine Densford. If you wanted to devote your life to a nursing career, you simply did not marry! Of course, the same was true of school teachers."

Hortense continued then to tell how the student nurses were assigned to various hospitals in the Twin Cities so that they

George McKay family at Gull Lake. Front row l. to r. father, George M. McKay, brother Wallace, sister Mabel McKay Gilbert, mother, Lydia McKay. Back row, l. to r. George R. McKay, Peter G. McKay and Hortense E. McKay, summer 1949.

12

could get special experience to study and observe nursing more closely.

"I well remember spending some time at the University Hospital, the Minneapolis General Hospital and the Tuberculosis Sanitarium at Glen Lake. There were certainly differences between hospitals and doctors in those days. Dr. Peyton, in his democratic approach to medicine, was an outstanding man."

I added, "I always thought that your maroon capes were most attractive, and your little white caps always looked so clean and starchy to me."

"In my senior year I had bad luck," Hortense said. "I broke my leg! That delayed me from graduating with my class. Times were bad, the big depression, so I too was unemployed for a while."

Bob sympathized. "A broken leg, 3 quarters behind your graduating class, and no job! You were off to a bad start, but at least you had your nursing degree soon."

Our ardent conversation on nursing was interrupted when amiable Dr. Jack Echternacht, our Chairman, rattled a water glass with his fork to quiet us. Our speaker was a sparkling young woman named Nancy Devine, a representative from the Minnesota Alumni Office in Minneapolis, who spoke to us on our role as friends of the University.

"Divine!" I whispered to Hortense. "Now that's an appropriate name for a public relations person."

Hortense smiled back. "I remember a nurse Miss Hurt at one of the hospitals. She was a pain!"

Bob laughed, "Once in a while a joke helps the digestion, especially for an old duffer like me."

On our way home from the meeting, I said to Bob, "A nurse surely has to keep smiling, always surrounded by illness and death. I don't think they ever receive enough credit for all their concern. Their whole life's one of service and compassion."

"I've heard that she served with the US Army nurses at Bataan and Leyte," Bob said. "So she's not the usual kind of nurse, nor the usual kind of person. Better write down some of her stories if you get a chance."

13

Hortense with little white cap as a student nurse in uniform. University of Minnesota, 1933.

SEVEN YEARS OF NURSING IN THE USA

For a short period of time, Hortense, Marion Dimmick (also a U of M graduate in Nursing) and I worked elbow to elbow as volunteers. From long computerized lists, we tried to verify the current addresses of the thousands of University of Minnesota Alums residing in Crow Wing county. Updating is similar to a lost and found column, only it involves people. There's no better way to become acquainted than through this kind of volunteerism.

As we were checking through the members living at Deerwood, Hortense said, "Deerwood. That reminds me, one of my first nursing jobs was right here in Crow Wing County at the Sanitarium in Deerwood, only about twenty miles from here."

I said, "Tuberculosis is one disease we seldom hear about anymore. Hurrah, for the discovery of new medicines!"

"In those days, it was still prevalent. Realizing that Caroline Walz, the County Nurse, could use some help, I often went to the rural areas with her to give Mantoux tests (TB) as well as the usual eye, ear, throat and hearing tests for the school children."

"I suppose at that time there were still many one-room schoolhouses," I said, thinking of the big bell in a school tower.

"Indeed! Most of them had a wood stove, and an old pump and outdoor toilets. Being a schoolteacher in those days had realistic problems, some of which were solved by the County Nurse."

Yet another day, we reflected on how many alums had died or moved away, and how many millions of letters each year must end in the Dead Letter Office. Missing letters have been known to lose sweethearts, and even battles that changed the course of history. That made us feel how worthwhile it was to find correct addresses.

After our Alumni project was completed, Hortense and I rewarded ourselves with a rich piece of pecan pie at the Sawmill Inn. I was determined as a woodpecker to have her continue her life story.

"Hortense, where did you practice nursing after you left the Sanitarium at Deerwood?"

"I worked for a short time in the Public Health Service at Louisville, Kentucky. From there I was transferred to Galveston. I soon discovered that things were a lot different in the South. The trip down there was stifling. There was no air-

15

conditioning on the train and the soot flew in everywhere through open windows. For the first time I saw Negroes on the train segregated from the Whites. In the streetcars too, first they stopped to pick up the Whites and then a few hundred feet further, they would stop and pick up the Blacks. In the shoestores, the Whites sat up in front and the Blacks in the back against the shoe stacks. In delivery trucks, the White man drove and the Black man went along to assist him. The beaches at Galveston were segregated too, and, of course, the patients in our hospital. Most of this has changed now."

"Did you go tarpon fishing on the Gulf?" I asked, remembering a few days I spent at Freeport.

"Yes, and we had great fun crabbing along the beach."

Now I ordered more coffee so that my friend would continue with her life story.

"The year that the Nazis invaded Poland in 1939 was a tense time. It was then I was transferred to the US Army Nurse Corps at Fort Benning, Georgia. This hospital was a larger one with approximately 200 beds. That winter it expanded because of a respiratory epidemic of pneumonia and flu. In those days, we treated these diseases with sulfanilamide.

For the first time at Fort Benning, I saw hospital patients who were <u>not</u> segregated. Doctor Kirkpatrick, our ward doctor, said, "We're taking care of sick people here, and we're not concerned about their color." An air of benevolence existed between Blacks and Whites. Around Eastertime, a small jazz band of Negroes came to our nurses' quarters and gave us a lively concert, somewhat in appreciation. We all abided by the Christian philosophy of goodwill. Few of us had any idea that we would soon be waging a war for human rights, the right of every human being to walk in freedom and dignity."

"Why did you decide to join the Army in the first place, Hortense?"

"The need for nurses was great; the opportunity for advancement was obvious. Of course, I believed in human justice. Within a few years I was sent overseas."

"Won't you tell me about your years as a nurse in the jungles of Bataan and Leyte?" I asked, sitting with renewed interest on the edge of my chair.

Hortense replied, "Come over to my apartment next Thursday and I'll fill you in on the rest of my story."

So it was that for a number of Thursdays we met at her apartment, which contained insignias, "dogtags" and other framed memorabilia about happenings the likes of which few women have ever undergone. I listened to some of the incredible ordeals of US Army nurses, those women of valor, who served freedom's fight in the Pacific Area. Having experienced the Japanese attack on Clark Field, the horrors of starvation at Bataan, a daring escape from Corregidor, and the care of the wounded and dying at Leyte, Lieutenant-Colonel McKay narrates her own story in these succeeding pages.

Maxine K. Russell
Brainerd, Minnesota

PART I
McKAY STORY

DESTINATION: THE PHILIPPINES

On February 20, 1941, along with two other nurses, a few officers, doctors and a number of troops, I arrived on the USAT Grant at Manila. With me, riding down in the ship's hold, was my faithful Chevy coupe. On coming into the port of this very large city, just fourteen degrees above the equator, the intense heat of the tropics was pervasive. I was wilted by the humidity. My short hair and clothing were sweaty and damp. Directly upon landing, some of my shipmates and I were assigned to the army hospital at Fort Stotsenburg, closely adjoining Clark Field, about sixty miles north of Manila. Enroute, my guide was Jessie Locke. She pointed out the hazards of getting through this jumble of Filipino traffic. Having had no previous experince driving on the left hand side of the road, I really felt that I was lucky to get us there without an accident. Almost instantly, I had to reverse my driving habits of a lifetime.

In those disturbing times, the danger of World War II was imminent. Certain precautionary preparations against Japan were in progress. The grim bombings of Pearl Harbor were only ten months ahead.

So here I was, an army nurse in the Philippines, about thirty years of age then, rather small of stature, but fully dedicated to serve the sick and dying. Having lived my childhood on two family farms, one at Harmony, Minnesota (where I was born), and later at Brainerd, Minnesota, I must have learned a few survival techniques from my nearness to nature. It wasn't many months before I would be tested in the jungle for courage and endurance.

I had had previous limited experience in the treatment of some of the tropical diseases, such as malaria, typhoid, dysentery, beriberi, hook worm and other related illnesses generally prevalent in warm climates, having spent some time in hospitals in Minnesota, Texas and Georgia.

When we first arrived at Fort Stotsenburg, we nurses took time to explore the countryside in order to learn more about the Philippine ethos - the people, the culture, the attitudes, colorful costumes and foods they ate. We drove across the surrounding

US Army Transport Grant loading coal in Hawaii and regularly transporting troops and supplies to Manila. 1941.

US Army nurse Hortense McKay arrives at Fort Stotsenburg in Pampanga, P. I. in February 1941, with her 1938 Chevy coupe. The car was a war casualty.

20

2nd Lt. Hortense McKay, left, and another US Army Nurse, Jessie Locke, right, at the Army and Navy Club in Manila, Feb. 22, 1941. While at Bataan 13 months later, Hortense's usual weight of 115 pounds dropped to 88 pounds because of starvation rations.

21

hilly terrain where rice paddies were cultivated and picturesque beasts of burden, the carabao, were much in use. However, as war threats in the Pacific gradually became more critical, our liberties were restricted. There were alerts. Permission to leave the Post was withheld. This was just a small forerunner of what we nurses would have to go through in the days ahead.

I was the only woman from Brainerd at the Post. Within a few months, however, there were many men from the Brainerd area, perhaps a hundred or more, some of them to die later on the Bataan Death March. I happen to remember the names of a few: Herb Strobel, John Falconer, Ed Burke, Clint Quinlan and Walt Samuelson. Once we nurses invited some of these Brainerd men from the 194th Tank Battalion to dine with us in our rather posh quarters. You see, we had our own Filipino male cook ("Dodo" by name), and two houseboys and a Filipino woman called a "lavandera" who laundered our clothes. The Philippine-grown rice, camotes and prawns, and the delicious ice-creams of papaya, pineapple and mango, were a memorable feast in lieu of the starvation for all of us yet to come.

The vegetation around us was lush and beautiful. Flame trees, palms, bamboo, banana, hedges of crotons, night-blooming cerus, gardenias and orchids surrounded us everywhere. Sometimes I would reflect on my childhood near Harmony, Minnesota, with its many wild moccasin orchids in the big woods near our farm.

From time to time, Chinese vendors would come to our quarters to sell fine embroideries and even rugs. Some of these pieces of embroidery were made by Filipino girls who had been taught by the Maryknoll nuns to do this fine work on pineapple fiber and linen. One weekend I drove up to Baguio, the summer capitol quite some distance north of Manila, intending to visit Sister Isabella, a Maryknoll friend of mine. Unfortunately she wasn't there. I became acquainted then with some of the other sisters. My last contact with them was Christmas morning when I phoned them to see how they were surviving and let them know my whereabouts. Most of these nuns were Americans so I felt a kinship for them.

Once a band of Negrito Pygmies came down from the mountains west of the Post to receive their allocations of rice. They carried long hunting spears, maybe five feet long, and demonstrated how they could be used. These tiny people from the Zambales Mountains were less than five feet tall. They appeared to be friendly and intelligent. They lived a very primitive life in these mountains which were visible west of the Fort. Because of the good will established here, they came again later on during the war. This time they carried a Japanese prisoner. I've never seen such a strange sight in all my life! They had this fellow bound round and round with native vines until his neck and head were the only things left untrussed. What a skillful bandaging job! No nurse could have been more thorough. He couldn't have escaped if he were Houdini!

Also at Fort Stotsenburg, because of the dampness, our conventional housekeeping was difficult. The chicken feathers in the pillows stunk to high heaven as damp feathers do. There was no polyester then. We lighted 25 watt bulbs in the closet for our clothing and shoes. If we left them just anywhere, in no time flat a green mold would grow over the leather. To keep my radio operating in this moist climate, I had to keep it in this "dry" closet.

It was here at Fort Stotsenburg that I had my first ride in one of the *first* jeeps. Drab green with a four-wheel drive, it was a good challenge in rough jungle terrain, far better than motorcycles with sidecars. The jeep was a very versatile vehicle endearing itself to the troops. Prior to the war, there were very few jeeps. I also remember at that time that Ed Burke and his crew took Willa Hook and me for our first ride in a tank. They were so proud of their tank, almost like kids with new toys.

But why were there so few supplies in our Pacific area? It's unfathomable to the average person today how our supply lines could possibly have been so weak. Of course, the distance was great; the ships were slow. The airplanes were scarce, even though more new B17's were being flown out across the Pacific. Our weapons too were very scarce considering the imminent conflict. We also had very few medical supplies, soap, paper products and other manufactured goods. Of course, it was prudent not to be oversupplied on some things because of the rapid deterioration in tropical climate. Now, cleanliness, the washing of hands, the covering of food with nets, and the boiling of water for dishes were among the nurse's best weapons against disease. Later, it would be prayer.

As I awakened the morning of December 8th, I suddenly heard over my radio that Pearl Harbor had been bombed. Over and over again, this message was reported continuously. Everyone was stunned. We felt that *we* would be next. Immediately

23

the first order given us nurses was to discharge almost all of our patients from the hospital. The officers felt that most patients would be better off with their own units. Fortunately at that time, there were very few seriously ill soldiers. I remember having one case of amoeba in my ward about which the doctor had previously joked, "If I sit in front of the microscope long enough, I might find *one* amoeba in this fellow's specimen." Perhaps some felt they would be safer in the hospital.

I had another patient recovering from an appendectomy. He was in his 8th day under hospital care. Naturally this was before the days of early ambulation. When the first air raid sounded, he jumped out of his sick bed, and when the bombing began, he leaped over the railing outside. It was almost comical. I never saw him again. Under extreme stress, some patients get well mighty fast. As it happened, he would have been safer in the hospital.

It was about noon when the first bomb fell. Clark Field had its own "Pearl Harbor!" I'll never forget this first attack by the Japanese. Air raid sirens continued to shriek through our wards. The planes began to descend in droves. Now it was sheer terror for all of us.

As the Japanese continued to drop these heavy loads of bombs, there was very little resistance on the part of our forces. The eastern sky was as black as the center of a tornado. The bombing was followed by strafing, all of it devastating and horrible. They hit unbelievable numbers of our planes, most of them brand new, our barracks, our shops almost completely demolishing the field with explosion and fire. Smoke and flames shot into the air. I lost all sense of time. Later, our adjutant, Donald Smith, told us that the Japanese had attacked us for three hours. Strangely enough, our hospital wasn't hit. It was only a very short distance, a block or so adjacent to Clark Field. Perhaps there were some traitors among those inside? You can imagine though our anguish and concern that our hospital would be bombed. It never was.

Immediately after the bombing, our previously empty hospital filled up with the wounded and dying. We nurses weren't prepared for such casualties, hundreds and hundreds of them. Bodies of the wounded, dying or dead were set on the porches, some on litters, some on the ground. Wards were overfilled. Many died right in front of me. It was blood-chilling! Some men cried out for help; others were completely silent, too stunned to speak, and there were those who said,"Go on to someone who needs it more than me." Many of them were ripped apart beyond recognition. I remember seeing one soldier die in bed, his bleeding so profuse that it completely soaked through the mattress. Others like him hemorrhaged so badly that they never had a chance.

Unfortunately, in those days, there was no plasma or whole blood to cope with this catastrophe. The need for medical help was desperate. My mind kept saying "Dear God, help me save lives, help me save lives." We couldn't allow ourselves to despair. The urgency was so great that there was hardly any record keeping, great gaps in the records or no charting at all. We put signs on the foreheads of some of the badly wounded telling what drugs we had given them, what morphine dosage and the like.

One soldier called me Hortense by name, but his face was so badly burned that I didn't recognize him. It was all so horrible- so many died- so many without arms, without legs. Everywhere around me were lives to be saved and so few of us to save them.

The entire medical staff was utterly overwhelmed with exhaustion. In desperate need, dentists became anesthesists or served in surgery. After the initial attack, the headquarters at Manila must have finally realized, or been appraised, that we were in urgent need of help, and at last, close to midnight, help came.

Once the magnitude of the damage, death and injuries was fully known, then teams of doctors and nurses from both the Army and the Navy arrived and worked endlessly round the clock to operate on and care for the injured. Temporary hospitals had to be set up as civilians from the surrounding countryside came for medical help. Everyone worked as fast as possible to save lives.

And yet, during such tense hours when surrounded by stark tragedy, there always seemed to be something light-hearted to help us keep our sanity. It so happened that one of the nurses who first came up from Manila brought her golf clubs along. Everything had happened so quickly that she simply had no idea of the massive extent of the bombings, destruction and death. She must have thought that she'd have time to go out to the Country Club! I guess a little comic relief at the sight of that golf bag was helpful to all of us in the face of this terrible disaster.

Many other posts in the Pacific area were bombed. Air

attacks came repeatedly. Our planes were badly damaged and there seemed to be no American planes to fight back. I heard later that half of the Far Eastern Air Force was destroyed on the ground in these attacks. Feverishly our soldiers continued digging foxholes and locating places to take cover. As more beds became available in Manila, our hospital was more rapidly cleared of casualties as they occurred. We somehow realized that a move would soon be necessary and so we packed and repacked our things.

Finally, on December 24th, something which we greatly feared, our big move to evacuate Fort Stotsenburg, happened. We had just put a big turkey in the oven to celebrate Christmas Eve, but we were never able to eat it. Believe me, it was not a Christmas tree Christmas. We received our orders to pack up at once. The entire post, with troops, hospital, everything, was to be moved immediately to Manila. It was a maneuver of urgency, speed and courage. The Japanese advance attack was on the way.

I loaded my Chevy Coupe with operating supplies, largely instruments and packs, and then accompanied by Lieutenant Lamey, we drove to Manila with Sternberg Hospital as our destination. All of these supplies, plus my car, were left at Sternberg Hospital. One of the nurses there, Edith Shacklette, kept my car keys for me. I was not to receive my keys from her until I reached Corregidor and they were no longer of any use to me. Another one of life's little ironies! My Chevy was destined to be a war casualty.

Some of us were instructed to go to the Spanish Club. There was a very large hall inside, and we slept on the dance floor. The only luggage I had with me was a musette bag, much smaller than a hat box. The next morning was Christmas Day. Imagine spending it, some of it at least, in the Jai-alai Club! The entire game-playing floor was covered with empty beds awaiting casualties. Also in this Jai-alai Club, there was a restaurant where we were to take our meals. One of the nurses, Willa Hook, and I sat at breakfast with two doctors, Wade Robinson and Donald Smith. One of these men couldn't swallow. He was completely choked up. These doctors had just received their orders to go to Bataan. What a Christmas present!

A short while later, we nurses received our orders to be ready to leave in 15 minutes. When I inquired about taking my Chevy, I was given a definite "no." My poor car! I never did see it again.

Everywhere the tension and suspense was enormous. But this short 15 minute departure turned out to be a farce. I sat around and waited hour after hour with two other nurses, Mollie Peterson and Gwen Lee. In fact, we waited all day long until 8:30 P. M. when finally we were taken to the port area to board a small ship. Half of us had already boarded when suddenly the air-raid warning went off. The alarmed captain, in order to protect his ship, cast off leaving half of his passengers and cargo on the pier. What next! After a time, seeing that it was a false alarm, he returned for the rest of the bewildered passengers, and then we finally set out. That was my Christmas, waiting and wondering where I was bound for and when the next disaster would strike.

Enroute, we could see the fires from Cavite caused by our oil tanks burning. They most likely had been set intentionally in order to deny our oil supply to the oncoming enemy. At nightfall, Manila looked uncanny, and somehow made think of Rome burning. These fires were so bright in the darkness that we probably could have read a newspaper on deck.

At dawn the next day, we arrived at Corregidor, the large fortress on "The Rock" where General Douglas MacArthur was in command. This great fortification was once known as "the Rock of Gibraltar of the East." It was the largest of the islands at the entrance to Manila Bay, and it was 3 1/2 miles long and 1 1/2 miles across at its widest part. Here we slept at Topside Hospital. At that time there was a move on to get the equipment, supplies and patients out of Topside and down into the previously designated Malinta Tunnel Hospital.

The main tunnel at Malinta was large enough for a railroad track and train down its center. It was about 1400 feet long and thirty feet wide with 25 laterals. Simply huge! For many years, supplies had been secreted away in these many pre-planned tunnels constructed for just such anticipated purposes.

The entrance to the hospital was on the north side. It had twelve laterals. I'd never seen a tunnel hospital before. For some patients as well as nurses, it was a claustrophobic experience. Some joked and said they had "Tunnelitis." However, ventilation at Malinta was a real problem. Stale air and bad odors pervaded, especially in the hospital tunnel. At times the power failed, and the noisy air blowers were always turned off during an air attack. What a strange anomaly it was for me, a nurse, to work in a 1000-bed hospital under 400 feet of solid rock with bombing and a war going on outside!

Many dignitaries had previously arrived at the fortress. I saw them all. Among them was the President of the Philippines, Quezon, and his family and staff. With a lap rug over him, Quezon was often wheeled outdoors for fresh air by one of his staff. President Quezon was afflicted with tuberculosis. He happened to be outside not far from me during one of the bombings. I watched him quickly throw off his lap robe, abandon the wheelchair, and all on his own, rapidly disappear into the tunnel. It was amusing but frightening as well.

Other dignitaries present at "The Rock" were US High Commissioner Sayre and Mrs. Sayre. She was an artist, a very good one, who frequently sketched the surrounding scenery. I also saw General and Mrs. Douglas MacArthur and their dear little four-year-old son, "Little Arthur," with his little red wagon and his "Amah" who took care of him. Mrs. MacArthur was a most gracious lady. She would visit the wounded in the hospital quite regularly. At one point, I remember her offering to help us nurses. Bless her! She was very sympathetic to the staff as well as the patients.

Yes, I saw them all, particularly the women and children in their day to day personal behavior. There was one toilet, only *one*, set aside for all the women at the hospital end of the tunnel. This included the presidential party, the high commissioner's party, the nurses and a few of the officers' wives. Imagine only *one* toilet for all these people. This is shocking to someone accustomed to good standards of plumbing. I could say more on upbringing, selfishness and personal hygiene, but I think that would be unprofessional of me.

Suddenly one night one of the ladies had what I believed to be a miscarriage. She was extremely ill. Eventually, because of starvation, shock and fear most women and nurses, with very few exceptions, stopped menstruating.

I worked here at the tunnel hospital in Corregidor for about 4 weeks until such a time as I was transferred to Bataan. Before leaving Corregidor, we had a very bad air attack - tons and tons of bombs in just a few hours. Stretchers filled with the wounded came into our lateral. It would only be a matter of time now before "The Rock" would be subjected to more and more aerial bombardments.

Malinta Tunnel Hospital entrance under 400 feet of rock. Picture taken before World War II.

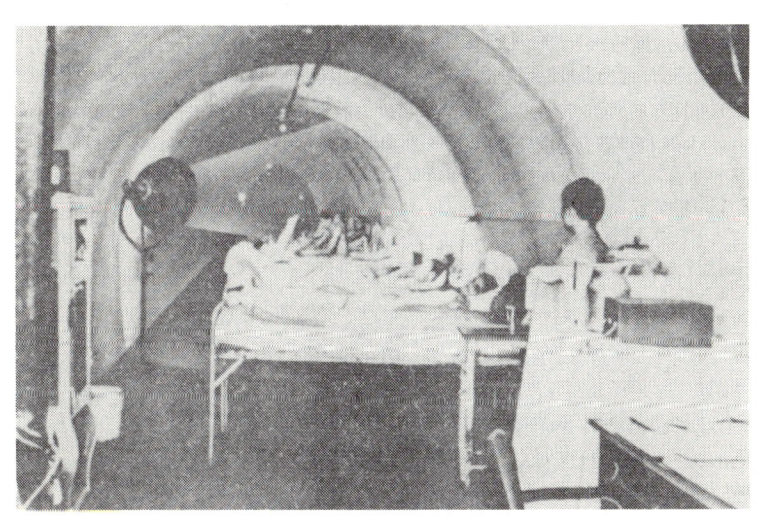

Malinta Tunnel Hospital. A small section of the 1000 bed hospital where 2nd Lt. McKay was a nurse. 1942.

29

BATAAN JUNGLE

I traveled to Bataan on a very small rowboat, the kind that had an outboard motor attached. There were only about six persons in our party. I felt like I was a tiny speck floating on the ocean surrounded by a macrocosm of jungles. Luckily it was not the rainy season, but it was excruciatingly hot.

There were two hospitals at Bataan. Hospital One was at Little Baguio, where the elevation was higher and where it was somewhat cooler. Also, Hospital One was reputed to be better supplied and laid out. It had a cement floor which was easier to clean and work on. But I was sent to Hospital Two, which was completely out-of-doors, unprotected from the elements and of lower elevation. In the daytime, most of the patients were out in the sweltering sun, except for some very limited shade. At night they were under the stars. However, Hospital Two had one big advantage. It was near a little stream for bathing and washing clothes. What a lifesaver it was to have this water to relax and refresh us! Even so, sometimes we were overly tired and very discouraged.

I took my turn on night duty, generally twelve hours at a stretch. At times, I had to walk in total darkness. I could hear strange noises of jungle animals. We were cautioned about the green snakes that hung from the trees. A camouflaged color, they looked very much like vines and bamboo. The sharp bamboo often scratched us. Frequently little Geckos, small transparent four-legged lizards with suction-cup feet, plopped down in front of us quite unexpectedly. Big rats would scramble around and between the bamboo. It was all a bit frightening. One day a big cobra shot by a GI was passed around the camp. We knew these poisonous snakes were all around us, but to touch one, even a dead one, made us all the more apprehensive of our location.

We had a great number of patients in Hospital Two who suffered from stress neuroses (once called shell-shock). Some of them left their beds and ran around disorientated in the darkness. What horrible mental spells these men must have endured! I remember one Filipino soldier who had cerebral malaria. He was out of his head. For his own protection, our soldiers had to build him a kind of "cage" out of boards in order to constrain him.

Army nurses bathing in Real River, Hospital #2, Bataan. Hortense McKay is the nurse with her side to the camera, wearing a fatigue uniform.

Outdoor Hospital #2 in the jungle of Bataan where Hortense McKay was a nurse. 6000 patients here before April 8, 1942.

Some of our patients slept on hospital beds, some on canvas cots and others on mattresses on the ground. Later, for extra beds, we used mattress covers filled with bamboo leaves. A few old "Pambusco" buses were hauled in for added shelter for the nurses' quarters. Untold energy had already gone into preparing this entire layout before my arrival- the motor pool, the pharmacy, the mess hall, operating rooms, toilets and other overwhelming needs of a jungle hospital.

In the beginning, most wards had about three hundred patients. The big problem was the hot sun. The only covered shelters were a few canvas ones under which we kept our office and other supplies. But as the sick and wounded kept coming, we literally ran out of space. Our hospital became larger and larger stretching out within and beyond the original area for hundreds of feet. Our facilities were taxed to the extreme.

Treated water went into canvas Lister bags which had spigots at the bottom. Imagine 300 or more persons trying to get drinking water from just a few bags! It was impossible. Some persons simply went without water until the next fill. The water from the Real River stream was used for bathing, but it was completely unsafe to drink.

I recall watching two Filipino soldier-patients of mine working their own assembly line. One had lost his right arm and the other had lost his left. They worked together as a perfect team stretching and folding bandages. Out of dire need, most soiled bandages were washed and used over again.

There were a great many amputees. As they recovered, we nurses encouraged them to try to do as much as they could for themselves. I remember giving Chuck, whose right arm was missing, a small 3 by 5 inch mirror. I helped him get started, but soon he learned to shave with his left hand and doing it very well. Most amputees were resourceful.

As our food supplies were gradually consumed and we received fewer or no replacements, we began to starve. My usual 115 pounds dropped to about 88 pounds. There were about 6,000 patients in our hospital waiting to be fed. We went on half-rations, relying more on rice than protein. Also, we were out of quinine. Many of our GI's died of malaria and dysentery, both known as the great killers. However, some were disabled but survived. The wounded who had "gas gangrene" were an added care. There were various parasitic diseases, such as round worms, both endemic and epidemic. How shocking it was to us

American nurses to have the experience of finding patients with large balls of worms in their stools! And there were overwhelming numbers of flies, spiders, ants and other insects which thrived and abounded everywhere in this thick jungle.

Our outside latrines were repulsive and soon filled with millions of maggots. At first, sand was sprinkled on the excreta. Upon urination, the sand would wash away and now the maggots by the billions would appear all over again. Then, the Sanitary Corps poured oil over them, but soon we were out of oil. With so much dysentery, most persons had "accidents" on their way to the latrine. As the maggots appeared along the paths on the ground, the flies and mosquitoes landed and carried the dysentery all over the area. In this jungle heat, the stench was terrible. When the toilet paper was almost gone, we could only give everyone two small sections with a tiny piece of soap. Most relied on nature's leaves. It was so ridiculous that at times we would laugh, however tragically, about the awful inadequacy of such a situation.

The fast growing bamboo was very useful to us. The Filipinos had long used bamboo in a great many ways. We began more and more to respect its versatility and adapt it to our needs. For example, it was used along with vines for bed frames, benches, clothes lines, tables in the mess hall, mats, drinking cups, cigarette holders and for shelters. Another unusual use for bamboo was the construction of frames to fit over the latrine holes in the ground. These frames were built in a rectangular shape. One bamboo bar was used as the seat and another bar was used for the person's legs. Jungle conditions had made everyone of us unusually resourceful.

Even so, it became more and more obvious that if help didn't come soon we would all starve to death. I was in charge of feeding 90 people from a 12 quart bucket. The contents were a strange mixture, a kind of "Bataan stew," with maybe some mule or horsemeat, carabao, even monkey, perhaps fish, rice and occasionally a few green weeds or maybe vegetables. Someone had jokingly put up a sign: NO SECONDS. The food bucket, with a piece of bamboo through the handle, had to be carried by two persons. We always put netting over the food because the flies were everywhere. It was difficult to keep the food clean. We did the best we could. Salmonella, fecal streptococci and other pathogens of intestinal origin could be deadly to many already weak from too little food.

33

We had to be scrupulously careful to give each person his fair share, the exact amount, even down to measuring *teaspoons* of something. Only a few months previous to this starvation diet, I remember the Chief Nurse, Florence MacDonald, saying "It's a sin to overeat and it's a sin to waste food, but I don't know which sin is worse." Starving people I thought must be without that sin. They didn't have either choice to make. There was little enough one could do for all these suffering and emaciated soldiers.

As the saying goes, "There's no atheist in a foxhole." I had with my belongings only two books, the **Bible** and a copy of Emerson's **Essays**. Both of these books helped to calm me, both remained behind on Bataan. As I daily witnessed the courage of amputees, I tried to live by my favorite Emerson quote, "What a new face courage puts on everything!" We nurses tried our best to keep our outward expressions as cheerful as possible. Diaries were forbidden, but sometimes I wrote letters to my family which were never sent. One picture could have told a thousand words, but there was no film available to those who had cameras.

Casualties flooded into our area. By one estimate, there were now close to seven thousand. We had fewer and fewer supplies to fight the enemy, and we were practically defeated by sickness and hunger. Just as Bataan was falling into the hands of the Japanese, all of the nurses were ordered to be transferred at once back to Corregidor. We had no idea what our future destination would be. After months of shelling and bombing, we wondered if we could make it through the jungles. Colonel Vanderboget, our commanding officer, had been seriously injured. Major McCloskey and some of our medical officers had been killed. Verbal orders were given by our Chief Nurse, Josie Nesbit, at General Hospital Two that we were to leave for Corregidor promptly at 8:30 P. M.. I believe it was April 8, 1942.

To some extent we made our own arrangements to get back. Beulah Putnam, Beth Veley and myself, all of us weak from hunger and fever, started out together. Beulah knew a reliable soldier-driver in the motor pool from Sternberg who could get a vehicle. En route, I remember getting out of the car which was stopped by the congested non-movement of troops. There seemed to be thousands of them. Weak and exhausted, I leaned my head up against a tree and everything was swimming before my eyes. That evening, I had taken some luminol, about three times the proper dosage, and I was quite ill as a result. In the melee surrounding us, we could hear the small arms shooting through the jungles. We knew that the Japanese were advancing.

By this time it was dark, I could hear people calling out for each other into the night. Some columns of men were marching in the opposite direction from us. One of these men was a Filipino Scout from Stotsenburg Hospital. And how loyal these Scouts were! Upon hearing women's voices, he enquired in English, "Who are you?" When I told him who I was, he said he thought he recognized my voice. We exchanged a few heartfelt good wishes of concern and yet another parting took place. This passing in the night, this crowded road through the jungle, it was all so eerie and frightening.

A great many vehicles broke down. Most of them were loaded with people, the cars without gas and later abandoned. Our sedan also broke down. Then, Beulah, Beth and I were lucky to hitch a ride with two Air Corps men who were headed for some destination in the mountains. The radiator of their car leaked so badly that we had to stop constantly to cool the motor and try to locate more water. The many troops and all the confusion and congestion delayed us. Our soldiers were dynamiting ammo dumps. It sounded like the rumble of thunder. There were flashes of flames in the background. After many paralyzing hours of waiting and then driving on through the jungles, we finally reached the shore. Beth Veley was especially disabled with a severe case of malaria. She suffered with nausea and was shaking with chills and fever. It was then I recognized Colonel Josiah Worthington, the veterinarian who had sailed with his family to Manila on the USAT Grant the same time as I did. That was fortunate because he made a real effort to find space on a boat to take us to Corregidor. We were collapsing with exhaustion. It had been dusk when we left Bataan, and now it was dawn of the next day when we arrived here at the beach near Mariveles Landing.

Just a few hours later at about 8 A. M. that same morning, our boat reached Corregidor. I remember one of the Military saying "My God, look at them!" Up to that time I hadn't realized how terrible we looked. Emaciated, pale, sick and weary, our clothing torn and soiled, we must have astounded him. However, above all else, I was grateful to God. Somehow we had made it out of the jungle on an *angel* wing and a prayer. We didn't know what fate had in store for us. I suppose the

35

Command had decided that our usefulness as nurses would be greater on Corregidor than as prisoners at Bataan. With heartbreak, we realized that we had left thousands of the sick and wounded behind us, but these were our orders. I would have to live with this tragedy for the rest of my life.

We were assigned at once to augment the nursing staff at Malinta Tunnel Hospital. Additional space had been created in the "dog leg" of the hospital by the gradual departure of the MacArthurs and other dignitaries. Here we heard many sad stories of brutal stabbings, beatings, and mutilation which had recently happened on the mainland, and the awful news of the much-dreaded Japanese advances across Luzon. General Jonathan W. Wainwright was now in command. It was this US General who gave the nurses the title of "Angels - the Angels of Bataan and Corregidor."

THE VALIANT MEN OF THE USS SPEARFISH

During the evening of May 3, 1942, thirteen of us women (11 army nurses, 1 navy nurse and 1 navy wife) were taken on a small boat through the Japanese minefields to a designated spot about three miles beyond the Rock of Corregidor. The harbor perimeter was surrounded by the enemy. It was a death-defying journey, the most frightening of my entire life. Should the slightest thing have gone wrong with the timing, the submarine would never have been able to wait for us. We might all have been drowned.

The USS Spearfish, in fear of a Japanese entrapment, was listening and waiting. Our small boat on approach winked a weak signal. To get from the boat to the sub, we had to feel our way in the dark, groping for railings and helping hands. Then we climbed through the hatch and down a ladder.

One of the crew members looking back at Manila said he saw the searchlights from Japanese-operated shore batteries. Quickly after the passengers (a total of 27) had embarked, the submarine submerged to the bottom where it waited quietly for 22 hours before attempting its escape. The Spearfish was under the command of Lt.. J. C. Dempsey (later, Rear-Admiral Dempsey, a distinguished submarine hero who twice received

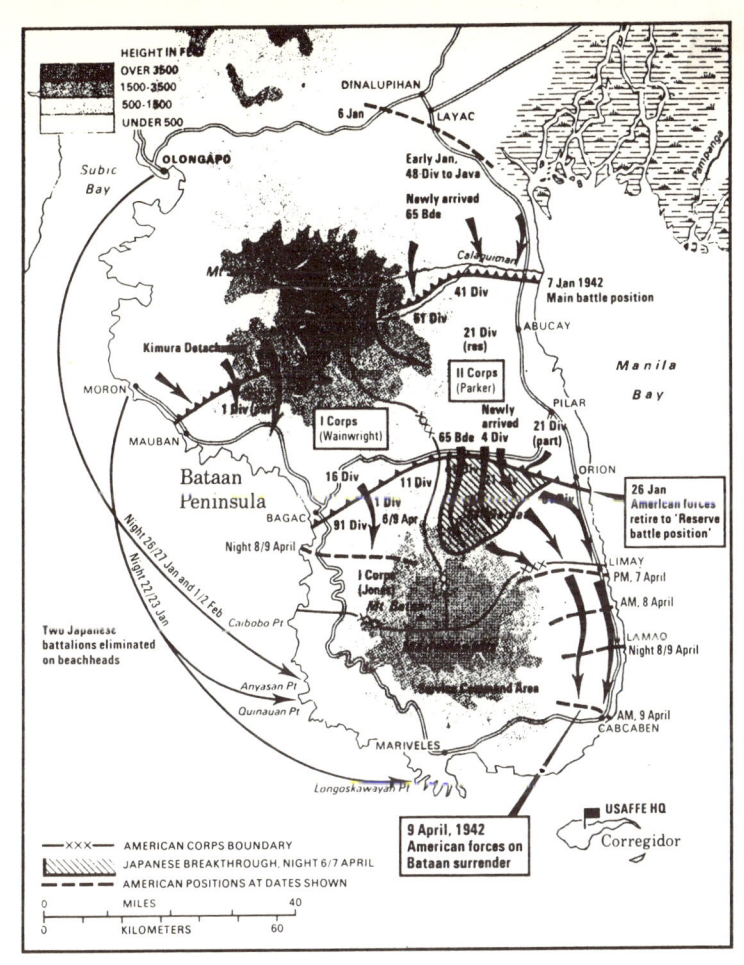

Map of Bataan Peninsula. April 9, 1942 Bataan surrendered to the Japanese.

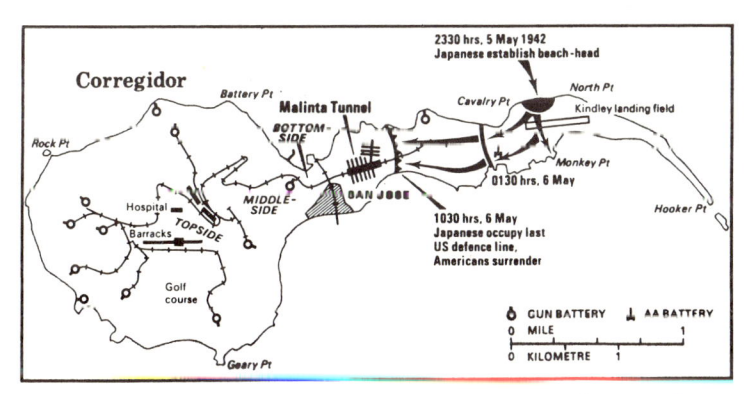

Map of "The Rock" Corregidor, May 6, 1942 Corregidor surrendered to Japanese.

37

2nd Lt. Hortense McKay was one of the 27 passengers rescued by the submarine, USS SPEARFISH from Corregidor on May 3, 1942. Lt. J. C. Dempsey, later Rear-Admiral Dempsey, received the Navy Cross for this daring mission.

the navy cross). We were thought to be the last Americans to leave Corregidor. Thirty-six hours later, the Japanese captured the Rock.

The interior of the sub seemed extremely complicated to me. Everywhere on walls and ceilings were pipes, gauges, faucets and controls. We were warned not to touch anything and keep out of the way. There truly wasn't enough room for an extra shoebox! The Spearfish was in no way equipped to handle all of these extra passengers.

In case of a depth charge, we were told to cover our heads with a pillow or blanket. A klaxon horn was used to signal a change of levels for a dive. Surface ships could "ping" to locate submerged subs. We were also told about periscopes, echo sounds and radio devices for spotting. We were now traveling from the South China Sea to the Java Sea through enemy waters.

When we crossed the equator, in spite of the fact that there was a war on, we passengers were treated to a little hanky-panky (in Navy parlance). Each of us was sent a special invitation to be initiated into "the best sports" group. King Neptune and his Queen presided. The Royal Doctor handed each of us an extra-large Royal Pill, with the advice to *take our pill and swallow it!* It was great fun to help lighten our journey and get us better acquainted.

When our sub passed Bali, yet in enemy territory, the commander could see lights on the shore. My admiration for these valiant men, the submariners, will never cease. Years later back in Minnesota, I was made an honorary member of the Viking Submarine Squadron.

On our 17 day journey to Fremantle, Australia, all of our ventilation system had to be turned off whenever enemy ships were above us. At such times, the heat became unbearable. I observed a crew member after such an experience wringing his own perspiration out of a previously dry bath towel. It was up to us not to move around too much because in doing so we would be using up vitally precious oxygen.

Along with the "buddy system," we also used the "hot bunk system." There were only four bunks for all of us 13 women in the chief's quarters where we slept. Each nurse would sleep 8 hours, then turn her bunk over to another nurse. We bathed with water condensed from the walls of the sub. The plumbing facilities were so complex that a crewman had to be put in charge. One nurse had remained in the cramped quarters for 15 minutes because she couldn't operate the water closet. To show you that her dilemma was real, here were the posted instructions for operating "a head":

> "Before using see that bowl flapper valve "A" is closed, that gate valve "C" in discharge pipe line is open, and Valve "D" in water supply line is open. Then open Valve "E" next to bowl to admit necessary water."

All of this detailed maneuvering would have been quite a ceremony for anyone with dysentery.

    As we neared Australia, our sub began to run on the surface during the daytime. Temporary excitement occurred when a plane was sighted. Then our sub had to put out a signal to verify its identity. Even though we passengers felt danger might still occur, we were reassured that land was near by a crew member who proceeded to press his blue wool suit in anticipation of his shore leave. He wanted to be ready. We were sure he knew something we didn't know. In turn, we felt it wouldn't be long and we would be leaving the sub at Fremantle.
    The following poem was given to me at the end of our journey. It was written by a member of the submarine crew.

What Women Can Do To A Submarine Crew

Beyond a doubt
You'll surely note
if you walk about
a change in the boat.

"Swede's" drinkin' coffee
"Beast's" turned to tea
"Pushover" keeps buffin' up
as pretty as can be.

Scanlan's smokin' cigarettes
Pettit's washin' clothes
and even our dear Yeoman
stopped pickin' his nose.

"Joey's" up and about
all his time off watch
hanging round the mess hall
playing the music box.

I'm tryin' to say in all these verses
we brought aboard some pretty nurses
on that eventful day in May
when we were out Corregidor way.

-anonymous crew member
USS Spearfish SS190

AUSTRALIAN INTERLUDE

With deepest gratitude to Lieutenant Dempsey and the crew of the Spearfish, I was now in Perth, West Australia. Perth! How strange I thought that it was from Perthshire, Scotland, that my grandfather Peter McKay emigrated to America about a generation ago!

Subsequently, we were taken to the Hotel Esplanade. It was heaven! Good clean sheets, a hot tub bath and all the luxuries of a first class hotel! I wasn't there long, only a week, just time enough to eat delicious and abundant food and to catch up on my sleep between *fresh sheets*! Some nights I experienced bad dreams. I suppose that they were "fear" dreams for my patients and fellow workers and what dreadful things might have happened to them as prisoners.

The news about the successful battle of our aircraft carriers in the Coral Seas had a positive influence and jubilance upon all of us. This battle was crucial in stopping the southern expansion of the Japanese. However, in the North, the Japanese had made definite advances over the Owen Stanley Range of New Guinea. At that time, I still had no idea of the extent and horror inflicted upon our sick and starving soldiers in the long Death March at Bataan.

As was expected, the two navy women left us for destinations under Navy jurisdiction. The US Army's Chief Nurse, Mary Bateman, at the 5th Station Hospital in Perth, assisted the rest of us. She saw to it that all eleven of us were able to get warm clothing before we set out on our long train trip across the Outback for Melbourne.

For six days, we would be traveling on a troop train. Some Australian soldiers had been brought to Perth from the Middle East. Our car with compartments was in the middle of the train. We were in the company of two US enlisted men who were sent along to manage some lockers taken out of Corregidor. We surmised that they probably contained military records and other valuable documents. There were many train cars packed full of troops to the front and the back of us. Our compartment doors opened only to the outside, not to the front or the back. It was a long train. Our only opportunity to see the troops from other cars was outdoors when the train stopped.

For the most part, we were supplied with limited rations of

hard tack and bully beef. No meals were served on the train. However, some good fairy had placed some extra oranges and raisins in our compartment along with a few extra blankets. Boy, was it cold! I suppose, since we had just come from the tropics, our blood wasn't up to par. Winter was approaching. The Australians seemed to stand the cold much better. We nurses had to sleep two to a bunk. That was a bit amusing and sometimes a bit annoying with someone else's feet in my face.

Occasionally the train stopped for water. At such times, the Australian troops were permitted to go outside, and all of us might be served hot tea. The Aussies simply dipped their cups right into the big pails of tea. No one behaved with tea party manners.

When we arrived at Kalgoorlie, a gold mining town of about 9000, we stopped long enough to visit a couple of stores. Rationing had commenced. Their stock was depleted. We had a little Australian money with us so I bought a yard of yellow-checked gingham to make a towel and washcloth. It was too light weight, but it would have to do. In the kitchen of a downtown hotel, we were able to buy some sliced beef. It seemed that most of the time all of us were *hungry*! We had not yet recovered from our pangs of starvation.

And now the journey to the East was across very flat and barren land. There was much desertlike brush and dried out river beds, and almost nothing else as far as the eye could see. Once, as we sped along, we passed a crew of Italian war prisoners working on the railroad tracks.

At one of the train stops, five or six aborigines were waiting to trade with the passengers. I traded an orange for two boomerangs, each of them about 15 inches long. We were told that they were somewhat crafty people. No aborigine would have bartered away a perfect boomerang. Both of mine were flat on one side and convex on the other with imperfections along the edges. They used these boomerangs for hunting. These people were dark-skinned with dark fuzzy hair, of average height, and they whispered among each other a great deal. The Australians told us that the aborigines had an unusual ability as skilled trackers. If someone was lost, they could tell if that person had passed by a week ago, two weeks ago, or even a month earlier by the smell of the tracks, the appearance of the soil and other skilled observations.

I never thought I'd ever ride in a caboose (although raised in

Brainerd, I'd seen plenty of them). The train crew must have taken a shine to us I suppose because they invited some of us nurses to ride in back and help them make a stew. And, of course, we were always hungry. I remember what a treat it was peeling potatoes, carrots and onions, and then with a chunk of soup meat cooking up a delicious stew on their little stove. But, ah, me!- as the day wore on we couldn't find much in common to talk about. It was difficult to understand their accent, and with nothing to read, no cards to play, nothing to do, our conversation lagged. The scenery was wearisome, mostly flat land with spots of Gum. I guess I was still suffering from fatigue because I slept for miles until the next train stop when we headed back to our compartment. Anyway, it was the first and last time I've ever had a ride in a caboose.

When we arrived at Adelaide, three-fourths of our journey was over. Here the gauge of the railroad tracks changed so we had to disembark to get on another train. Some of the American officers of the 41st were staying over at a hotel there. They *saw to it* that we nurses missed our train by giving us the wrong information. The rascals!

So it actually took us seven days to get to Melbourne, which was a very large city of about a million and a half people. Since we were expected a day earlier, Ann Fellmuth, a former Sternberg Hospital nurse, couldn't imagine what happened to us. She had gone to the station twice to meet us. That took a little explaining. Ann Fellmuth was outfitted in the new Army Nurses' blue wool uniform, which looked mighty attractive to us. The first thing that she warned us about was *don't talk to reporters*. Ann had arrived in Australia some time earlier on the Mactan with the most seriously injured troops evacuated from the Philippines.

The Mactan was an inter-island steamer which was never built to be a hospital ship. The Red Cross had procured this ship to bring the many American and Filipino casualties to Australia. It was at a time when Manila was being declared an open city. Most of the evacuated casualties were from Fort Stotsenburg, Fort McKinley and Sternberg General Hospital. The ship proved to be a far safer place than Corregidor. However, conditions aboard were very taxed. There were very few trained personnel on this ship, and there were some very, very sick soldiers. The Mactan is a story in itself. Ann described it as a harrowing trip. Amongst the survivors was a soldier who had his buttocks shot off; another one so badly burned he was never expected to survive. Miraculously, both of these young men *did* survive. In spite of the grave dangers of the war at sea, the Mactan made it to Australia with the majority of its patients alive.

It was here at Melbourne that we nurses were taken to the USA 4th General Hospital (a Western Reserve Unit) for our physical examinations. Being fit for duty, I was given the option to stay or to return to the USA and be reassigned. I chose to stay.

One afternoon I met two of the nurses who had preceded our group. They had been evacuated by plane from the Philippines and had stayed on in Australia. These women came down to Australia through Mindanao and Darwin. They had equally terrifying experiences to relate. We went together to a tearoom where we could talk. We were served some delicious date scones with whipped cream on them. I can still taste their richness. What a luxury that was! This was before more austerity measures were imposed on the Australians. Sometimes on evening walks, we tried to locate the four bright stars of the Southern Cross constellation. Star watching at night was a soothing recreation. How micro-small we are against the vast universe!

For a short time until reassigned again, I was at the 4th General Hospital for duty at the Port Dispensary, Headquarters Base Section Two, as their nurse. Here's the way admissions generally worked: the patient was first sent to the Dispensary, and then only if sufficiently ill or diseased, to a General Hospital. At the Port Dispensary one day, I was working with three young doctors just newly arrived from the States. They knew I'd seen service in the Philippines and many air attacks with terrible casualties. With a big smile, one of them said to me, "Well, what do we do now, *Boss?*" This comment was rather the reverse of the usual doctor-nurse relationship. War will do this. At least theoretically speaking, the nurse has been considered closer to the patient than the doctor.

At first while I was living at General Hospital, we would be driven back and forth to the Dispensary in an *ambulance!* One fellow passenger carried his guitar and we'd all sing along with him. "Waltzing Matilda" was generally a favorite. Anyone seeing us singing and riding along in an ambulance must have thought we were "bonkers!"

Later while still in Melbourne, I was housed with SWPA

Headquarters' nurses. We lived in a fashionable Toorak Road residence. About this time, I met a man from St. Paul, Minnesota, a quartermaster officer, Morton Katz, whose background was the meat packing business. He told me that he would never forget how much I ate. He'd seen people take seconds, but never one who took *thirds!* That's what starvation can do to you. Morton Katz was a graduate of the University of Minnesota in the same class I believe as mine. In the late seventies, he left a bequest, the residue of his substantial estate, to the University of Minnesota. In my many experiences as I've moved about the globe, I've found that one of life's greatest joys is being able to pick up the threads of friendship. Meeting the Katz family in St. Paul later after the war was over has proved to me how precious are these threads of friendship.

A SALUTE TO SYDNEY

After three months in Melbourne, I was assigned to another Base Headquarters in Sydney, New South Wales. This city was somewhat larger than Melbourne. Even though I had traveled to many places in and about the Pacific, it was a particular privilege for me to live in this beautiful city of Sydney for the next two years.

The city has a deep harbor, one of the finest natural harbors in the world. In such a setting, there were views all around me - the coves, the beaches, the rocky escarpments and the heads through which I could see the incoming ships. One morning there was a rumor afloat that the liner Queen Mary was coming into the harbor, and when she did, how overwhelming it was to see her size! At that time, she was used as a troop ship, sometimes carrying as many as 15,000 troops. There were many yachts, sailboats, ferries, tugs and all the endless fascination of ocean traffic in a big harbor.

During these years in Sydney, I was in Administration (a part of the Office of the Base Surgeon). My duties were diverse. My role, in general, concerned itself with the nurses and the nursing service including dieticians and physical therapists. Housing was critical. There was rent control. All billeting (lodging to the lay person) was controlled by a Billeting Office. We needed to be sure that our nurses lived in suitable quarters. Some rental places in Sydney, as in all big cities, were too remote or too far from public transportation or perhaps in questionable neighborhoods. Our office made every effort to assure these women nurses a pleasant leave from their forward assignments. Another duty of ours was meeting the troop ships upon their arrival at the port and subsequently orienting these women in Theater Area policies.

Recreation was necessary too. A trip to the zoo to see the koala bear, kangaroo, wallaby and wombats might be a real delight for them. Shows and movies were fun too. I recall once that General Rilea loaned us his motor boat so that we nurses could see the city of Sydney from the harbor side, indeed a very beautiful experience.

As part of the surgeon's staff, we made periodic inspections to the various hospitals under our jurisdiction. On one such trip, I saw Eleanor Roosevelt touring the wards of one of the hospitals. Her knitting bag was always close at hand. She was a very friendly, industrious and dedicated First Lady.

There was also a Black Unit (at that time called Negro) which was taken into the US Army Nurse Corps. Birdie Brown was the Chief Nurse of this unit. Australia itself was predominately Caucasian; so too before World War II was our Army Nurse Corps. Until this time, we had had no Negro Hospital Unit sent to our Theater. Deserving Birdie Brown was to be commended for what was a particularly difficult position. With boredom and impatience, this unit had to wait for assignments from the North. Delays of this sort were bound to create problems. These Black nurses had come to make a contribution, and they were happiest when busy and taking care of patients.

It was most important that the women nurses wore clothing that fit and felt right. It helped us maintain our "esprit de corps." During the time I was in charge, we were going from wools to cottons. Some of our clothing did come from the USA. However, under the reverse lend-lease program with Australia, there was local fabrication with numerous sizes available. It was a difficult task to find our women sufficient clothing for tropical wear, as, for example, the right head gear, the right shoe sizes, ankle length slacks, long sleeves, culottes and the like. Later on in the war, some Navy women arrived who had been already outfitted in the USA. There were no WAC's (Women's Army Corps) here in Sydney at that time.

So much of being a woman is associated with individuality and style. Some styles are alike, such as copying the proper skirt length; some are different, such as the angle of a cap or a flower in the hair. Nurses had to be in uniform and that posed some problems. We had to change our life style and give up dressy clothes and jewelry. If the word went out that some nurse was seen dancing (perhaps at the popular Prince's Night Club) without her cap on and a gardenia in her hair, the next day the rest of us would be reminded of this regulation: Women are to wear head gear in public places at all times (certainly no frilly flowers or jewelry).

As part of the Australian Austerity Program, you couldn't spend your money no matter how much you had. There were strict limitations. Four shillings was the top price for breakfast, five shillings for lunch and six shillings for dinner. For more varied food, people began arranging dinners in private homes hoping for a tender steak, a good salad, and plenty of fruit. However, these places were not food inspected so they were a real risk. So many people were hungry and still they couldn't buy anything for their money.

In some ways, American and Australian social customs differed. Once the Aussie nurses invited us American nurses to supper. We were told to be there at seven. Well, we were. Then, 8 o'clock came and went, and then 9 o'clock and 10 o'clock, and still there was no sign of supper. Finally, at 11 o'clock, all of us ravenously hungry, we were served SUPPER!

In parks, in offices and on trams, it seemed that the Australian women were always knitting. We American women at times would watch them carefully to see if they were dropping stitches. We couldn't comprehend how they could talk, notice the scenery and knit elaborate patterns all at the same time while riding on the tram, but they did.

Margo was one of the Australian women who worked in our medical office. In order to have a change of wardrobe, she went home over the weekend and arrived back on Monday morning with an entirely new sweater. She had taken the yarn off her old one and completely reknit it into a new one. As a female, always wanting a change of clothing, here was one way to get it, no matter how much effort it took.

The men had it easier because they were in the majority, and the Army was long experienced in outfitting them. Such was not the case with women's clothing. There were no stockings, culottes, slacks, Kotex, Bobbie pins and other much-needed sundry items in the shops. Just imagine such shopping conditions! Women had to put up with many more shortages than men.

Two friends who meant a great deal to me while in Sydney were W. J. and Phyllis Dawes. Their home was always open to me. In general, the Australians were extremely kind to us Americans. They appreciated what we did for them in the war. Sometimes Phyllis would bring me little treats of food, namely, two precious chicken eggs ("chooks" she called them) fresh from their henhouse. Sometimes it might be just six delicious strawberries or a cluster of roses from their garden. Nothing could have been more appreciated. Phyllis Dawes was the sister of Dr. Wil Johnson, my minister, back in days before the war when I was working as a nurse in Galveston, Texas. Once again here in Sydney, I was able to pick up previous threads of friendship. Like a loom weaving colorful patterns, all through my life it seems that new situations and old threads of friendship have been constantly meeting, emerging and changing.

For some months now, our US Army had been "leap-frogging," as we called it. Troops were gradually being moved further North. Most army troops at Adelaide and Melbourne were being withdrawn. There was continuous movement. Some persons left because of assignments or other duties; some left to go on leave; some because of illness. If you were only slightly injured and able to get back to duty within a month, you were kept on; but if, for example, you lost your leg, you'd be sent back to the States. People were constantly coming and going. At last I too had my orders to move North to Australian New Guinea.

My last night in Sydney I had a wonderful surprise. I was entertaining six nurses in my tiny one-room apartment close to Wynyard Station when suddenly the phone rang. It was my youngest brother, Wallace McKay, a signalman in the US Navy. He arrived about 8 P. M. just as we were finishing dinner. He must have been able to convince his superior officer in Brisbane that he really *did* have a sister in the US Army. There were jokes around about men wanting leave who gave phoney excuses. I hadn't seen Wallace in four years. After he barged into my small apartment filled with six army nurses, the place was really packed! One of my guests was Colonel Nola Forrest from Pipestone. Strangely enough, I would see my brother again in Hollandia, Dutch New Guinea, at Christmas. Again, quite by chance, I met him a third time at Leyte in the Philippines. How happy my mother was to learn later that we had not only met once during the war but *three* times!

49

SIZZLING - HOT NEW GUINEA

Some of our generals didn't want women in the military services at all, not even women nurses. They didn't want the problems of having women around. The larger and more exciting the city (like Sydney) the fewer the problems. When I was sent up to Port Moresby, New Guinea, there appeared to be a great many problems. It was extremely hot, less than ten degrees below the equator. Life here was dull. There were large units of women in a specially built camp nearby who were housed and kept until they were able to join the male components of their own units. Sometimes as many as 600 women would arrive here at one time. These women were in a foreign place with no amusements, no games, no libraries. Idle women confined to a limited geographic space were like the unemployed. They lost their incentive, and so there were many resulting problems.

Since it wasn't possible to keep all the troops up front, these women nurses became part of the service troops in the background. They had to be "staged," moved on in progression, or taken away to relieve the congestion. Such situations are difficult for civilians and soldiers alike to understand, particularly those impatient ones who want to get in and get on with the war. In some ways, conditions were perhaps similar to those in the movie, M*A*S*H (Mobile Army Surgical Hospital). That was Korea, but here in New Guinea, there was extremely rugged terrain, sweltering heat, plus innumerable islands and the Coral Sea.

Before many days past, I found myself traveling by plane from Port Moresby across the Owen Stanley Mountains to Cape Sudest. There were two fuzzy-wuzzies on our plane. They were nature boys, wearing only the briefest of loin cloths and very colorful headbands. These primitive New Guinea natives had the respect of the Australians for their ability at Rescue and Jungle Survival. I wondered how these strangely primitive men must have felt to be flying across mountains and jungles high up in the sky in this new found age of the airplane?

When I arrived at Cape Sudest, Australian New Guinea, it was late November 1944. I was at that time on detached service to the Clothing Distribution Center Quartermaster at Headquarters Intersection, British New Guinea. Here I worked mainly with women's tropical clothing to see that there was a full range of replacement sizes. As an example, when baggage went astray, clothing replacements were necessary. We had to carry many sizes in high-topped women's shoes, anywhere from 5 B to 11 AAA. Clumsy shoes were nicknamed by our nurses as "Daisy Mays."

We weren't far from the equator so it was beastly hot here. We worked from 6 A. M. until 11 A. M. with time out for lunch (similar to a "siesta"). After that, we would return about 3 P. M. and work until supper at 6 P. M. Normally after supper, we'd go back to work again until 9 P. M., unless there was a movie or a church service. Our hours of work were dreadfully long.

When the WAC's (Women's Army Corps) arrived in sizzling-hot New Guinea, we women nurses were finally taken out of the Quartermaster Women's Center and assigned back to the General Hospital. At that time, I met one of the WAC's from my hometown of Brainerd, Minnesota. She was M. Eleanor Nolan, a Company Commander, and a lawyer by profession. She had been outfitted in the USA, and she chose to wear men's trousers. In this way, it might be said that she expressed her own individuality.

For a short time I was on temporary duty but assigned to the 126th General Hospital at Hollandia, Dutch New Guinea. Now it was hotter than ever - only 2 1/2 degrees south of the equator. We were told that General Douglas MacArthur and his petite wife, Jean, were in military residence. I worked here at Hollandia and waited for my orders to join the officers, troops and additional nurses farther North. At this hospital, I became very well reacquainted with the Johns Hopkins nurses. They had been trained at the noted Johns Hopkins Medical University. Again I had another surprise encounter here with my brother, Wallace McKay. Three of the Johns Hopkins nurses and I were invited to have Christmas dinner on his ship, the Henry T. Allen. It was a delicious treat and a truly happy Christmas for me.

Surprising events sometimes occurred. One morning I said goodbye to my friends from the Johns Hopkins outfit and within three hours I was on my way to the Emily Weder Hospital Ship along with a number of other nurses from #126 General Hospital. Up to this time, we had all been at various locations. My fond farewell was unnecessary. It was quite flabbergasting! All the Johns Hopkins nurses I had just said goodbye to were also on this ship, and we were all together again. That's how fast things sometimes happened in the Army.

THE HEARTBREAK AT LEYTE

Our hospital ship was once more crossing the equator and heading North for Leyte in the Philippines. En route, Peggy Carbaugh and I spent many hours together working ahead to evaluate the Nursing personnel for the difficult future assignment.

When we arrived in Leyte, it was dusk. Darkness seemed to come fast in the tropics. Our hospital ship was unloaded at night because the situation was dangerous. Those in command did not want the nurses to stay aboard ship for the rest of the night. As darkness descended, we were made to crawl down from the ship on netted ropes. Every nurse was given a number in order that each knew exactly where she would be placed for the night. It was extremely hot here and raining heavily. We were now just 11 degrees above the equator.

Because there were so many critically ill patients resulting from the Leyte Island conflict, the hospitals here were very active. Our group of women nurses were the first ones to arrive at the 133rd General Hospital. There were already patients in the beds. These wounded men had been temporarily cared for by corpsmen, but without nurses. We had to work with great speed. Everything was outdoors and under canvas. These facilities were being stretched to the limit.

However, almost incredibly within two weeks, the 126th General Hospital staff was sufficiently readied for our contingent. We women joined the male components to open under the command of Colonel Dismukes. I was the Chief Nurse in charge. Peggy Carbaugh, my assistant, who had had previous hospital experience in Australia, had been reassigned to a station hospital across the Palo River.

It rained intermittently night and day. The entire region was a jungle of mud. The engineers were constructing drainage ditches, but evenso, most of the beds were on wet ground. Imagine the condition of our shoes and clothing! To expedite things, because we would be doubling and even tripling our size, the medical officers would be out with the crews cutting down bamboo for new wards. Some persons criticized the doctors saying that they shouldn't be out in the wet jungle cutting bamboo. It wasn't professional. But they needed the additional wards desperately. The engineers had all they could do to clear the thick growth and put in roads. Since I had lived on a farm, I thought that I too could put in a spare hour of help clearing bamboo. I remember one of the engineers calling out to me, "Hi, Jungle Angel!"

Now, shortly afterwards, the first patients were transferred from the crowded hospital across the river where I mentioned Peggy Carbaugh was Chief Nurse. We were expanding continually. Some nights we would get in 200 or 300 new patients. The extent of their injuries was shocking! Arms missing, legs missing, deep scalp injuries, deep chest injuries, their faces all but destroyed! Unbelievable suffering! Our hospital grew and grew from 700 beds to 3300 beds! Thirty-three hundred beds of critically wounded and dying soldiers in the rainy, muddy, steaming tropics! It was certainly a nightmare!

In many ways conditions at Leyte were similar to those at Bataan except that we now had more and better food, medical supplies and equipment and the benefits of training became fully evident. By this time on Leyte, we had early triage, intravenous fluids and blood transfusions. Medical progress and our experience had changed the whole picture. Just the same, there were still a great many challenges to save lives.

In a very short while, our hospital began to specialize. Much of my work became administrative. We set up a women's ward of 40 beds. We also had a few isolated contagion wards for skin conditions like diphtheria. And we had all the polio cases on the island. At times our respirators and generators for polio didn't function well because there were such heavy electrical demands. Only two of the wards had cement floors for post-operative cases. The rest of the ground I repeat was muddy. There were a great many soldiers occupying beds in the neuropsychiatric wards. Although there was much genuine illness and suffering, for some soldiers it meant warm food, a bed, medical care and a glorious rest in contrast to combat areas which they left behind.

Ultimately, we had three wards of 80 beds each with Japanese prisoners. They were fenced in. When they first arrived, they were extremely emaciated. Gradually these enterprising prisoners began to express themselves in their own culture. They showed us their sense of artistic creativity. Out of salvaged material like disposable tubing from the hospital, they arranged a miniature garden with a little waterfall. Perhaps they were trying to show us their symbols of earth, man and heaven?

Early one morning, the night supervisor reported to me that

53

during the night we had received 5 liberated Americans who had been prisoners at Cabanatuan. They were in a very fragile state of health. Some were in such precarious state that they did not survive. When our soldiers saw the condition of some of these men, they would walk past their beds and quietly leave them a small gift - a pen, a piece of gum or some other simple thing as their token of understanding. Something within their hearts must have compelled them to do this.

One afternoon in February, the 126th adjutant came to tell me that there were 72 women coming to our hospital. Customarily I would have been prepared for that number. But now I felt certain that we had no room for 72 more women. However, upon further query, the adjutant said to me, "I believe these women have been prisoners, but I can send them on some place else." I responded instantly, "Prisoners! We will not send them on anywhere else. We'll keep them right here. We don't want them buffeted around from place to place." At that time, we were running *32 wards* and already taxed to capacity.

Having seen others break down under stress, I told my two assistants, Mildred Radakovitch and Marion Burkwall, that if they thought I was in any way emotionally unable to hold up, they should be prepared to take over my work. I had no idea how serious their conditions might be. Some terminal cases had come to us bloated by starvation and at the door of death.

However, when the 72 nurses arrived, sitting in trucks and waving at us with no litters and all of them able to walk, I was overjoyed. I knew them all. Eleanor O'Neill, the first nurse I had sailed with from San Francisco on the USAT Grant, was put up in my own tent. Nurses from our hospital and from the surrounding hospitals showed their true worth. They brought these liberated nurses their very best nylon bras, nighties, soaps, lipsticks and other personal effects. At such an emotional time, most nurses found something special of their own which they could contribute. These women prisoners had almost nothing but the clothes on their backs. I gave Eleanor my best satin nightie. She stroked the soft material and cried out, "Just think, we are free, free!" For us it was a most fulfilling experience to be able to do something for these long-deprived women. It was fortunate that we had recently built a Nipa palm hut for our night nurses to sleep in during the daytime. We were able to use these beds, a few more cots and any beds emptied by day sleepers. Many beds saw double duty.

These 72 women had been liberated from Santo Tomas Internment Camp at Manila. Even though the war was still in progress, they had been loaded onto a plane from Dewey Boulevard right in the middle of the street. It was a very bold rescue made by the 1st Cavalry Division. The story of these brave women prisoners is a story in itself, their story. In our hands now, they were given physicals, intravenous vitamins and other needed medical care. Some of their clothing was soiled, ill-fitting and without proper insignias because they had been out of touch during their imprisonment. We arranged for them to receive better clothing before they were sent back to San Francisco.

Busy as I was at this time, my brother, Wallace McKay, phoned one day hoping to see me before he returned to the USA. He had been selected to compete for the Naval Academy exams. Since his ship, Henry T. Allen, an attack transport, was near the Island of Leyte, my commanding officer, Colonel Dismukes, supplied me with a jeep and an armed driver. We planned to meet on the beach. It was getting dark. There were blackouts. The enemy was not far away. It was a tense situation. Just as I was about to leave with my driver, thinking that we would never get together, my brother jumped down before me from a "duck" (an amphibious vehicle). There was barely enough time for us to say hello and goodbye. Nevertheless, I was grateful for those few minutes with him. It was truly amazing I thought that I was able to see him again and for the third time in this vast Pacific Theatre of Operations.

OLD GLORY RAISED AGAIN

As time rolled on, the war seemed to lessen in our area. There was still limited fighting. Sometimes we saw "dogfights" from the air at close quarters. In contrast with the terrible annihilation we endured from the Japanese at Clark Field and Bataan, these flights over Leyte were for the most part our own USA fighters. With the advance of our troops northward to Luzon, we noticed fewer and fewer Japanese planes over our hospital. Gradually the hospital census diminished. The census went down from 3300 to 2300 patients. Just the same, we didn't close down any wards. Decisions of this magnitude rested with higher headquarters.

I should have mentioned earlier that there were very few registered male nurses. In fact, at that time men were not eligible for the Army Nurse Corps. Perhaps we might call it reverse discrimination. For the most part, these male nurses covered the convalescent wards which were lighter staffed. One of the problems was that from time to time in these convalescent wards, patients became sicker and sicker. Through the nurses' intervention, such patients would have to be moved back again to more fully-staffed wards.

The Red Cross Workers were another hard-working group. Mary Lesher and Chiyo Thomas handled the recreational activities and the many social problems. The dieticians worked with dehydrated foods and the physical therapists with rehabilitation. All of them contributed a great deal in meeting the constant demands of their various professional fields.

As conditions at Leyte bettered themselves, we women decided to set up a little beauty shop. None of us had seen the inside of a real beauty parlor for quite some time. Although we worked alongside men daily, we had none of the "ritual" of dating. Quite fortunately, we located a man in our unit who had had previous beautician experience. After interviewing him, to our delight we found out that besides cutting hair he could give permanents if we could supply him with 17% hydrogen peroxide. Through the ship's stores, we were able to obtain enough of the essential beauty products. You can well imagine that he was busy night and day! Now, that all of us nurses began to feel and look more beautiful and had a little more time available, the men in the surrounding units became interested in getting acquainted with us. Through the Red Cross, the Chaplain and myself (as Chief Nurse), it was decided best to screen the invitations for the women to visit the exclusively male units. Three of the most responsible unit women were assigned to take over this task force of "hearts and flowers." Here's what they did: First, a list was posted on the bulletin board with invitations, many very cleverly written. Secondly, the facilities for entertaining at these male units had to be properly described so that the nurses would know what they were getting into. Movies, singing, bridge and good food were all incentives to get the women to respond.

At the appointed hour, the nurses would leave our hospital

quarters by truck in a group accompanied by army officers who were entrusted to see them safely back again. Sign-out sheets had to be specific. For example, it was to be no later than 9 P. M., or 10 P. M., or perhaps 11 P. M., depending on the function-dinner, dancing, et cetera. One strict requirement was that the officers issuing the invitations had to have some kind of enclosure or "Day Room," not just out in the open jungle. For many, these social events were the beginnings of new friendships and romance. Sometimes these friendships developed into permanent relationships.

There were other happy moments as well for all of us. Famous people stopped off at Leyte. Irving Berlin with his wonderful music was there. A favorite song of mine by Berlin is **God Bless America, Land That I Love.** Recently I've read that he's still alive and 99 years of age. Joe E. Brown with his funny wide mouth and crazy gags put on a great show for us. Sometimes a symphony orchestra or a famous musician would perform. These visits by talented entertainers from the States helped keep up the morale of patients and staff alike.

One day Colonel Nola Forrest, our Theater Chief Nurse of the Surgeon Office, arranged for Peggy Carbaugh and me to be put on temporary duty at Manila. Old Glory was actually flying over the Philippines again. We accompanied her on tour to Clark Field and other large hospital centers outside Manila. It was difficult for us to look at the many war-torn ruins. Some of the big buildings had holes in their sides. Many of the bridges were gone. I kept one eye peeled open for a glimpse of my Chevy Coupe, but it was nowhere to be seen.

As we walked through the hospitals, I thought of the many people I had worked with here, wondering what had happened to them. Did they or did they not survive? I remembered thoughtful and kind things often done by the doctors, the kitchen workers, the nurses and the "lavanderas"- all small services but big in their own way. I thought of jokes and funny stories passed around the wards to make our days happier and help us overcome the fear we were vicariously experiencing for our very ill patients.

This trip back to Manila also revealed to me the miracle of healing. In spite of all the heavy bombing and strafing, I noticed that the bamboo and jacaranda, the acacia and oleander, and all the other green growth had rapidly begun to rejuvenate and bloom again. Red and green birds and brilliant-colored butterflies once more flitted about as they did before the war. I was happy to see that the rice paddies were being replanted and to note the large carabao once again being tended and splashed by the small boys. An yet, in the very heart of the city, there remained many battered buildings, damaged homes, warehouses and torn up roads, all the aftermath of heavy bombardment. God's green growth of jungle trees had renewed itself far faster than this man-made cement jungle of the city.

Since the war in Europe had ended in May, our supplies and personnel in the Pacific were now being diverted. Therefore, I felt it timely to request my return to the States. I was told that because of my many months of service overseas, I was entitled to leave at any time I wished. But I could not help but feel a deep sense of sorrow at departing. These tropical islands had offered me many beautiful experiences. I would never forget the many friendships made with the Filipino nurses as well as our own nurses, doctors and soldiers. In stark contrast, there were those awful days during the bombings. The reality of all that had happened, the many valorous deeds of the corpsmen and the doctors and nurses who worked around me, would always remain a part of me, close to my heart.

Sailing on a US Navy ship from Leyte back to San Francisco, I had time to reflect upon the war and upon life itself. As a nurse, I had learned to think beyond the blood, the maggots, the high fevers and the deep open wounds, and to focus upon the individual, the human being in his hours of trial. I had experienced many great miracles for human survival under the most extreme conditions. Some soldiers who appeared to be hopelessly mutilated in combat somehow miraculously improved and returned home to the States. We nurses always tried to encourage them in small ways *not to give up*. Often we had very few or no medical supplies. Sometimes what medicine we did have just didn't seem to help. It was then that a kindly touch and sympathetic understanding became important.

The art of nursing I thought is far more than medicine. It is a few words of encouragement, the squeeze of a hand, a refreshing bed bath and a kind glance. During those horrible hours of jungle warfare, we attempted to put aside self and self pity and substitute love for our fellow man. And in reply, a whispered thank-you from a very sick soldier, or a grateful look from the eyes of one dying, was all the appreciation and love we nurse ever wanted. Rewards come to us in quiet and mysterious ways.

TWENTY-FOUR YEARS OF SERVICE AS A US ARMY NURSE

Hortense McKay's years as a "Jungle Angel" in the Pacific area during World War II were over now, but not her nursing career. After she returned to the USA in 1945, she became involved in demobilization and the reestablishment of the Army Nurse Corps. New concepts in nursing began to result from the lessons which history had taught. To fulfill some promises that she made to herself, she went on to study at the University of Minnesota with an aim to improve methods and technology of army nursing. Along with the support and input of others, these changes would eventually result in the greater speed and efficiency with which nurses were able to cope in Korea and later in Vietnam.

A dossier listing her post-war achievements is noteworthy.

Chief Nurse, 12 state area, Headquarters 6th Service Command, Chicago, Ill., Demobilization. January 1946 until August 1947.

University for Minnesota, B. S. Nursing Education, graduate summa cum laude, from September 1947 until June 1949. To fulfill her promise to help in providing better training for army nurses.

Director, Department of Nursing, Medical Field Service School, Brooke Army Medical Center, Fort Sam Houston, Texas, to conduct courses and classes, first US Army Nurse so assigned. From July 1949 through December 1953.

Chief Nurse, Headquarters at Orleans, France, and Chief Nurse, in 34th General Hospital. This assignment covered all the US Army hospitals (5 of them) in France. It was during this period that the Army Health Nursing Service Program was initiated. February 1954 until May 1956.

Chief Nurse, US Army Hospital, Fort Eustis, Virginia, 150 beds, with emphasis on In Service, Education and Improvement of Nursing Service. May 1956 to May 1957.

Historical Writing, Historical Unit. She was the first army nurse assigned to this unit to gather materials for this history, "The Army Nurse Corps History from 1901-1958."

Assistant Chief Nursing Service, 350 bed hospital, US Army Hospital at Fort Ord, California, from Jan. 1959 to June 1960, at which time, after 24 years of service, Hortense McKay retired from the US Army Nurse Corps as Lieutenant Colonel.

Hortense McKay, BS Nursing Ed. , Summa Cum Laude, U. of Minn., Coffman Union in background. 1949.

Lt. Col. McKay receives her certificate of retirement from Col. Isiah Wiles. Note the hospital duty uniform and the then current Hattie Carnegie designed army nurses' uniform worn by Col. McKay. June 1960.

At Naval District Headquarters, Norfolk, Va., Lt. Col. McKay congratulates Rear-Admiral J. C. Dempsey, recipient of 2 Navy Crosses, upon his retirement.

On October 20, 1977, Lt. Col. McKay returned to the Philippines. Two principal events were included on this visit. The first consisted of many members of General Douglas MacArthur's staff attending the dedication of a monument depicting his landing on Leyte; the other was the memorial plaque on Mount Samat, Bataan, in recognition of the 27th Bomb Group. Some of the fiercest fighting of the war took place around this lofty mountain. Previously constructed along this slope was a tall white 300 foot cross. It was erected as a National Shrine to commemorate the 35th anniversary of the liberation of the Americans held prisoners of war in the Philippines. Fittingly, the Angels of Bataan and Corregidor were honored with a bronze plaque some time later. Hortense Eleanor McKay's name is listed along with 104 other nurses. The tablet at the Altar of Valor reads as follows:

US ARMY NURSE CORPS   US NAVY NURSE CORPS

IN HONOR OF THE VALIANT AMERICAN MILITARY WOMEN WHO GAVE SO MUCH OF THEMSELVES IN THE EARLY DAYS OF WORLD WAR II. THEY PROVIDED CARE AND COMFORT TO THE GALLANT DEFENDERS OF BATAAN AND CORREGIDOR. THEY LIVED ON A STARVATION DIET, SHARED THE BOMBING, STRAFING, SNIPING, SICKNESS AND DISEASE WHILE WORKING ENDLESS HOURS OF HEARTBREAKING DUTY. THESE NURSES ALWAYS HAD A SMILE, A TENDER TOUCH AND A KIND WORD FOR THEIR PATIENTS. THEY TRULY EARNED THE NAME-

"THE ANGELS OF BATAAN AND CORREGIDOR"

DEDICATED ON THIS 9TH DAY OF APRIL 1980

(The names of 104 nurses follow in three columns: In the center row, 6th from the bottom, 2nd Lt. Hortense E. McKay)

At the bottom of the plaque is the following statement:

WE ACKNOWLEDGE WITH DEEP APPRECIATION THE TWENTY PHILIPPINE NURSES WHO ASSISTED THEIR AMERICAN FRIENDS IN BOTH THE HOSPITALS OF BATAAN AND CORREGIDOR. THEIRS WAS A JOB WELL DONE. THEY WERE A CREDIT TO THE UNITED STATES AND THE REPUBLIC OF THE PHILIPPINES.

300 foot cross on Mt. Samat, Bataan, National Shrine to commemorate the 35th Anniversary of the liberation of the Americans held prisoners of war in the Philippines. 1980.

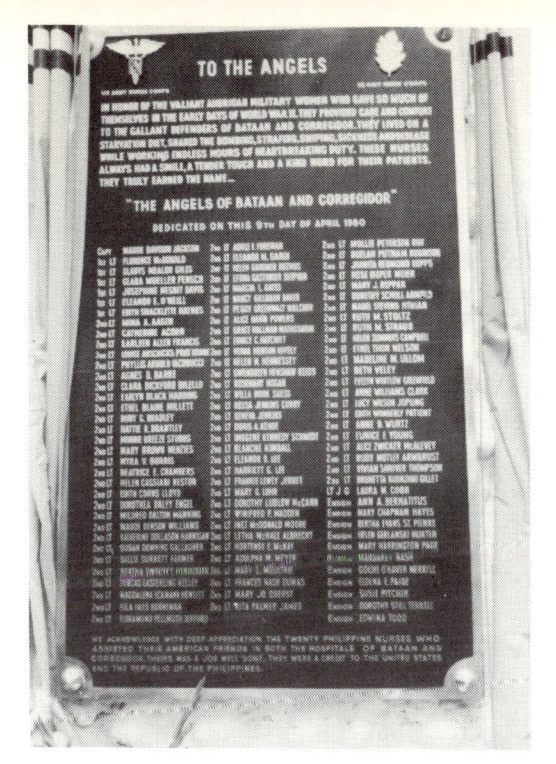

Tablet to the Angels of Bataan and Corregidor at the Altar of Valor, Mount Samat, the Philippines 1980. 2nd Lt. McKay is 2nd row, 6th from bottom.

Lt. Col. Hortense McKay decorated with the bronze star medal by Brig. Gen. John Cox, assistant Adjutant General Minnesota National Army Guard, for her participation in defense of the Philippines. Brainerd, MN Sept. 7, 1985.

THE CARILLON BELLS TOLL FOR HER

From the preceding pages, it's plain to see that Lieutenant Colonel McKay was one of Minnesota's outstanding women. What she experienced and achieved in those wartime years was far beyond what most women were able to do. As one of the "Angels of Bataan," she endured the bombings, starvation, anguish and heartbreak of the wounded and dying soldiers in the jungles of Bataan, and again, returning later, as Chief Nurse for a 3300 bed hospital in the jungles of Leyte. To the average person, the size of such a primitive hospital with wounded prisoners of war and dying soldiers is staggering.

At the end of World War II, this fearless woman assumed additional nursing responsibilities. As an example, Hortense McKay was Chief Nurse, 34th General Hospital, from February 1954 until May 1956. This assignment covered all of the five US ARMY hospitals at Orleans, France. What could be greater evidence of her capability to handle large assignments?

Upon her retirement in 1960, Hortense chose to live in the Brainerd area where her family once farmed. She was a nature-loving person who never lost touch with folks of the soil. She had many friends among the farmers in Crow Wing County, some of whose families went back to the year when she taught rural school there after some training at St. Cloud State Teachers' College. She would often listen to their views on farming and the plight of the family farm. Sometimes in the fall, with her close friend, Marion Dimmick, she would travel out to neighboring farms on a "potato gleaning" trip. After gaining permission, they would gather up the gleanings, "the best tasting potatoes of all," and turn them into elegant hot dishes, such as French au gratins or Swedish potatoes Supreme. With typical humor, Hortense said, "Marion, we're not "couch" potatoes. We're just field potatoes - the hard working kind."

One day in December, I met Hortense at Mills Fleet Farm with new brooms sticking out of her shopping cart. I asked her, "Why in the world all these brooms?" She bought them she said to give to the Paul Bunyan Arboretum. "Their brooms are all worn out, and I want to sweep up the pine needles in the workshed." She spent hours with Marion Dimmick and Rudy Hillig, the Arboretum Director, making Christmas wreaths. Rudy made the wreaths, Marion the bows and Hortense wired the cones and swept up the evergreen clippings. The same was true when she helped Marion to sew costumes for the Brainerd Community College Theatre productions. Like most nurses, she had been taught to work hard, and she never gave up her work ethic.

Considering her high rank of Lieutenant Colonel, she was indeed a very modest person. At the many meetings which she attended, her opinions were sought after; her comments were often inspirational. One of her AAUW friends said of her, "It was almost as if she were our social conscience." A member of her afternoon study group commented, "Hortense made an in-depth study of everything!" Yet another friend added, "She was a woman of courage, highly regarded by all of us." Without question, she had earned a special place in the hearts of those who knew her well.

Even though in January of 1985, she had had multiple (five) bypass heart surgery, she was not one to pamper herself. She was sometimes in discomfort or pain. Nevertheless, she continued to attend and be actively involved in the numerous organizations which she loved.

Together with Leola Buchite, Ellis King and other class members, Hortense participated for many years in her high school class activities. At her home on Lake Hubert, as late as last July 16, she entertained the Class of 1927 of the Brainerd High School Alumni at the 60th anniversary reunion. With the help of her brother Wallace and sister-in-law Margaret, there was a feast of "homemade" foods for over forty people.

As is the case with most nurses, Hortense had always been interested in proper diets. She was an advocate of health food dishes. She often baked her own bread, sometimes a blend of grains and honey, and she liked to make jelly from berries which she herself picked. Kiwi fruit jam was one of her kitchen creations. That she was once so near death by starvation at Bataan must have increased her awareness of nutrition.

Throughout her long nursing career, she had always helped and cared for people. She loved people. There seemed to be no end to her personal services. Just a few weeks before her death, she spent most of one afternoon and evening with a sick resident at Woodland Acres. Although she wasn't feeling well herself, she ended up late at night driving this friend to St. Joseph's Medical Center in order to spare her the ambulance costs. Hortense had spent a lifetime helping others, so in spite of her own pains, she was not about to let anyone down now.

She would have been delighted to know that her numerous affiliations were listed with her story. She was a life member of the University of Minnesota Alumni Association, a life member of AAUW (American Association of University Women), the Retired Officers' Association, American Defenders of Bataan and Corregidor, the Paul Bunyan Arboretum and the Crow Wing County Historical Society. In addition, she was an honorary member of the US Submarine Veterans of World War II, the Viking Submarine Squadron and Alpha Chapter 23 Order of the Eastern Star.

Life for all of us, like the last glorious rays of a winter sunset, has its own way of vanishing. On January 15, 1988, Hortense died at University of Minnesota Hospital while undergoing a second operation for heart surgery. In previous years, she had worked hard with others to restore the carillon bells in the Crow Wing County Court House. These carillons were dedicated to the 194th Tank Battalion and those incredibly brave men from Brainerd in the Bataan Death March.

On Wednesday, January 20, 1988, these carillon bells were tolled in honor of Lieutenant-Colonel Hortense McKay just previous to the memorial services. The Reverend R. Wayne Hardy, First Presbyterian Church, conducted the one P. M. service of worship. To hear the bells toll for our "Angel of Bataan" was for all present a deeply spiritual experience.

On the day that followed, Lieutenant-Colonel McKay was given a military escort by the Veterans of the American Legion Post 81 of Harmony, Minnesota. She was buried on a hill in Scotland Churchyard Cemetery near her parents. Pastor Wayne Hagen officiated. Two midshipmen cadets from the University of Minnesota were the buglers. Their commander read a poem from the Philippine War Memorial at Corregidor which Hortense had requested, "Sleep, My Sons." Across the winter landscape, there came a stream of sunlight and a chickadee's song. Someone very special, a great lady and a dear friend, was laid to rest.

*"Sleep, My Sons, Your Duty Done,
For Freedom's Light Has Come.
Sleep the Silent Depths of the Sea
In Your Bed of Hallowed Soil
Until You Hear at Dawn the Low Clear
Reveille of God."*

Lt. Col. Hortense McKay is buried at Scotland Churchyard Cemetery adjacent to this 125 year old Richland Prairie Church on the register of National Historic Buildings. Harmony, MN Jan. 21, 1988. Photo courtesy of Kay Dimmick

PART II
BATAAN REMEMBERED

To honor the heroic men of the Bataan Death March, those who survived and those who did not come back, in order that we Americans might live in a world of greater freedom and humanity. May the memory of their sacrifices always remain.

These are the members of the Brainerd National Guard unit who left here in 1941. Most of them wound up in Bataan and many never returned. From left to right in the first row are Carrol Guin, Fuss Swearingen, Pete Clabo, Bob Weygand, E. B. Miller, Scotty Muir, C. Quilan, Ed Burke, Art Root, C. Dunnell, Art Brown, B. Hyatt, F. Davis and Walt Samuelson. In the second row are F. Lowe, D. Karlson, B. Veillette, James Johnson, Harlan Peterson, M. Anderson, Glen Nelson, Walter Straka, James McComas, W. Goodrich, Donald Paine, Paul Searinen and Lee MacDonald. In the third row are H. Larson, Ken Porwol, H. Strobel, M. Dobson, W. Davis, W. Lackie, Art Thomas, Harold Snell, Bill Mattson, James Bogart, Ross Burrows, A. Brown, Bill Brown and C. Gilmer. In the fourth row are G. Roth, John Falconer, F. Friedrickson, Sid Saign, John Pederson, Art Gattie, V. Solsbee, Bud Carpenter, L. Alberg, P. C evenger, Ken Gordon, Bob Swanson, H. Finch and Frank South. In the fifth row are C. Tunner, Jim Clevenger, Jack Spornitz, Ray Fox, Wally Lee, Gus Bender, J. J. Allen, Mel Ahlgrim, Richard Davis, James Kerrigan, E. Gordon, Cliff Raridan and R. Hollingsworth. In the last row are G. Oliver, Carl Kramp, Henry Homburg, W. Bjornstad, C. Gonnion, E. Brusseau, H. Peck, Roy Maghan, Floyd Munger, Jack Jubie, G. Bell, Joe Lamkin and Roy Nordstrom.

71

There were 105 enlisted men and 5 officers, or a total of 110 men in Company "A" 194th Tank Battalion. Sixty-nine of these men later sailed on the luxury liner President Coolidge for the Philippines. Of these 69, 43 never came back. Brainerd lost 60% of its men, more than any other city of its size. These soldiers died in the Bataan Death March, the Hell Ships, and the POW camps in the Philippines and Japan. These Brainerd men, along with others, played a pivotal role in the outcome of World War II in the South Pacific. Through their stubborn defense of Luzon, they "threw the Japanese timetable for the conquest of the Pacific." The Japanese Army had made plans for victory as early as December 1941.

The 194th Tank Battalion fought from 8 December 1941 until 9 April 1942 when, under Major General Edward P. King, they were forced to surrender to the Japanese Imperial Army. The American and Filipino troops were without adequate ammunition and were overcome by disease and starvation. The Japanese had a strong army of over 300,000 fully equipped and well-trained troops.

"The 194th became a heroic legend by its series of rear guard actions. On the Agno River, 30 tanks and five halftracks from the 194th successfully held a 25-mile defense line. Isolated by impassable jungle, one platoon fought its way out of a tank trap, leaving the reeling enemy behind." (Taken from Historical Fact Sheet, Minnesota National Guard, Brainerd.)

"Of the original 85 officers and enlisted men that left Brainerd, Minnesota, 60 accompanied the 194th Tank Battalion overseas to the Philippines. Three men were killed in action during the encounter along the Agno River near Carmen on 26 December 1941. Twenty-eight officers and men died in prison camps prior to the end of the war. Twenty-nine of the original sixty who fought in the Philippines actually returned to Brainerd after the termination of World War II. " (from Historical Fact Sheet, Minnesota National Guard, Brainerd.)

Battle of Bataan

Sergeant Herbert Frederick Strobel, Nov. 14, 1916 - Dec. 26, 1941.

    Sergeant Herbert Frederick Strobel, 25, Brainerd, was the first death in the 194th Tank battalion, Company "A." The morning of Dec. 26, 1941, the Japanese troops tried to force a river crossing in the sector of Company "A." In the afternoon, they intensified their attack. About 2:50 P. M., a Japanese mortar shell struck the branch of a tree directly above the open turret of a tank commanded by Sgt. Herb Strobel. He died about 15 minutes later, a gallant soldier in the defense of his country.

    Hortense McKay's brothers George and Peter, and Herb Strobel attended high school together. They often played together in their boyhood because the Strobel family farm and the McKay family farm in Southeast Brainerd were adjacent to each other. One of the Strobels, Lenny, spoke of the father, George McKay as an intelligent, honest, and well-liked neighbor. He was also a very good whistler. "Early in the morning when he brought the cows into the barn, we could hear him, whistling as far as a half mile away." The two families were well acquainted and greatly grieved his loss. Herb was survived by his parents, Mr. and Mrs. J. F. Strobel, and his brothers John, Robert and Leonard, and sisters Bernice and Virginia.

    "Whosoever liveth and believeth in me shall never die."

John 11:26

THE HEROIC MEN OF THE BATAAN DEATH MARCH

Company "A" of the 194th Tank Battalion was a National Guard outfit comprised of citizen soldiers from practically all walks of life. The men in Company "A" were from the Brainerd area.

On or about April 9, 1942, these heroic soldiers, together with their commander Colonel Ernest B. Miller, fell into the hands of the Japanese Invasion of the Philippines. All of them were near starvation. (The nurses had been ordered out of Bataan on the 8th, the day before the surrender.) Now, there began one of the cruelest marches in modern times. At the point of Japanese bayonets, these many thousands of captives endured a five to seven day Death March of about 90 miles north from Mariveles to San Fernando. Some of the prisoners previously wounded were in a semi-delirious state; others collapsed from starvation, dehydration and heat stroke. If they attempted to stoop for a drink of dirty, slimy ditch water, or fell along the way, they were bayoneted to death. Filipino farmers who offered food to the prisoners were also bayoneted or burned to death with their bodies hung up as examples to others.

At San Fernando Rail Head, the survivors were herded into boxcars, the small oldtime "forty & eight" cars, with as many as 110 men to a car. Some of them died on their feet. All of them were near death from starvation, malaria, dysentery and asphyxiation. The filth of excrement and maggots clung to their bodies. After a death ride in oven-hot and "airless" boxcars, the survivors were again forced to march on from Capas to Camp O'Donnell, called the Camp of Death. They could scarcely drag themselves in the unbearable heat. At last, they were ordered to bury their own dead. It was a holocaust of torture. The stench of death was everywhere.

This brutal mistreatment of war prisoners was inhumane and senseless. How much Hell on earth can man create for man? Their cruelty and hatred was fanatical. This is only one of the horrible examples in history of man's fight for freedom and brotherly love. The Hell Ships that were to follow was yet another example of barbarism.

The loss of life in the Philippines was shocking. To illustrate the magnitude, there was a ration count for 80,000 persons before the Japanese Invasion on April 3, 1942. Later, after the

Death March April 10 - 16, 1942. Line of prisoners approached the end of the Bataan Death March. Improvised stretchers were used to carry those who were too weak to continue. Minneapolis Tribune

Brainerd soldiers on the Bataan Death March.
A Japanese Photo

Another view of our soldiers on the Bataan Death March.
A Japanese Photo

77

Invasion, there was a count of 63,000 men who survived the Death March and arrived about mid-April at Camp O'Donnell. At first the daily death rate was about 400; later, it became about 125 per day. Some of these prisoners were gradually transferred from Camp O' Donnell to Camp Cabanatuan.

Of these prisoners, there were 55,000 Filipino soldiers (who were defending their homeland); 8,000 of the prisoners were Americans; an additional 12,000 soldiers were missing. Over a period of time, 27,000 Filipinos were freed; 28,000 of them had been buried in mass graves. Of the 8,000 Americans, 4437 had died and were also buried in mass graves.* These figures are terrifying. Most of the remaining Americans (a few of them remained to starve at Bilibid and other camps) were taken as prisoners on Hell Ships to Japan where they were captives until the end of the War, VJ Day, August 14, 1945 and some months later.

As brutal as the Death March had been, the prolonged torture and unbelievable number of deaths on the Hell Ships was even greater. After about 40 days at sea, some ships which began with 1,500 prisoners in their holds arrived in Japan with only 400 or so. General Douglas MacArthur writing on the Hell Ships, said, "Of all the cases of brutality and mistreatment accorded prisoners of war that have come out of World War II, none can compare with the torment and torture suffered by our soldiers who were prisoners of the Japanese aboard the ships, Oryoku Maru, Brazil Maru and Enoura Maru on voyages from Manila to Japan during the months of December 1944 and January 1945."

*The statistics from the two foregoing paragraphs were taken from a book by Captain Paul L. Ashton, MD, **Bataan Diary**, with the permission of the author.

BATAAN REMEMBERED:
An Interview with Russell Swearingen

On April 6 1988 (almost 46 years to the day of the Bataan Death March), the author was fortunate to visit with a veteran hero of Bataan, Russell Swearingen, now one of only three survivors in the Brainerd area. The others are Walter Straka and Henry Peck.

Swearingen, a blue-eyed man of medium stature approaching his mid-seventies, is now quietly living out his life at Deerwood, Minnesota. Of "Pennyslvania Dutch" ancestry, he was born on June 27, 1914 at Groton, South Dakota. His mother died when he was only ten years old. After growing up in Missouri, Russell came to Brainerd in 1934 where he became established in the electrical business. In 1940, he was mobilized with the Minnesota National Guard 194th Tank Battalion Company "A."

However, little did Russell Swearingen realize then that he was destined to live through some of the cruelest experiences that men were ever forced to endure. "I'll never forget those days of marching as long as I live," Swearingen said, his face clouding with memories. "I was in the same outfit as Colonel Ernest Miller all the way. When Bataan fell to the Japanese Army, all of us were sick, exhausted and starving. The heat was terrible.

Then on April 10, 1942, we were forced by our Japanese captors to begin a 90 mile march north from Mariveles to San Fernando Rail Head. The officers marched right along with the men. There were thousands and thousands of us sick and starving. They gave us no food or water. They marched us right past the artesian wells. A few of us broke rank, drank from the dirty ditches, and then we were shot at or bayoneted to death. When we stopped marching at night, we didn't dare leave. I had no food for seven days. Finally, at San Fernando I was given a small ball of rice. After that, we were piled into hot steel sheds, shoulder to shoulder, and later taken from there into stifling railroad cars. Men died all around me, particularly those who had been seriously ill and weak from the beginning of the March. After reaching Camp O'Donnell on the 16th, I remember seeing a steady line of men at the barracks all day long carrying out the dead, sometimes 400, sometimes 500. The death rate was horrible. Some were Filipino-Americans, some were our men. About 1500 Americans died in less than two months. And when it came to our men digging all those graves, the soil was terribly hard - just like rock. There were flies everywhere. The water was terrible, and very little quinine and rice.

Some time after May 9th, we were moved to Camp Cabanatuan. Here we were divided into groups of ten men called "ten-men shooting squads." If one man escaped from this ten man group, disregarding the fact that he may have been caught, the other remaining nine men were executed. I witnessed two such terrible executions. Our men were first tied around posts, given the "sun treatment" and then beaten every hour when the guards changed. This went on sometimes from two to four days. Those guys were so badly beaten down that they were glad to be executed! On two occasions I remember that we were forced to watch them. It was really hard on us captives. A fellow prisoner- he'd been a neighbor of mine back in Brainerd- came to me really dejected. I tried to cheer him up, gave him two pieces of money I had on me, and said to him, 'Howard, get what you want with this. It'll help.' He said, 'Russ, I don't want to live. I just don't want to live!' Well, the next morning he was dead. Those fellows who talked that way usually didn't survive. Sometime in June, Captain Ed Burke, who had been wounded and missing, was brought to our Camp Cabanatuan. But he was one who made it back.

About the middle of November, I was sent to Japan on the same ship as Colonel Miller and some others from our outfit. It was a very old ship, the Nagato Maru. We were so packed into the ship's hold that we couldn't lay down, only squat. It was like walking in a cattle barn that hadn't been cleaned out all winter. Feces all over the floor! We were just like sick animals. Just a bucket of rice once a day for all of us. The rice was just like wallpaper paste, only thinner. After about forty days, there were only about 400 of us left out of 1500 or so. All of them were buried in the sea. My friends, officers Quinlen, Root and Guin all died on prison ships, called Hell Ships. The torture was diabolical, death and starvation.

When we debarked in Japan, it was very, very cold. I only had on my shorts. Coming from the hot Philippines, our blood was thin. Now once more we were marched in our weakened condition up to a camp. I was so sick and hazy that I had to fall out of line. Some American soldiers carried me for about a mile until I told them to save their strength and set me down. 'I'll try to feed on something,' I said. Then a group of Japanese officers came along and through an interpreter asked me what I was doing there. I told them I couldn't go another step. I was too weak. 'If you want to kill me, go right ahead,' I said. Then the officers told the interpreter that a truck that was going to the prison would pick me up. Well, they stopped and picked me up, and that was the only good thing that happened to me.

Only the strongest survived. First I had malaria, then dysentery, yellow jaundice, dengue fever, and in Japan I contracted diphtheria. Two men died in the beds on each side of me, but somehow I made it.

On or about January 20th, I was transported to Zentsuji War Prison Camp. I lost my eyesight. I was completely blind. My legs to the waist line as well as my arms were paralyzed. I didn't recover from this blindness for about 6 months, and the paralysis also continued on about 6 months. I tried to walk, to slide down stairways, and to hang along the walls outside the barracks, but I couldn't make it half-way to anywhere! I was told I had dry beriberi, a lack of vitamin B-1. I was treated with fermented rice like yeast. My bones ached. It was just like I had 50 toothaches in my feet. An extreme case. It was awfully painful. Lots of the fellows didn't make it. We were always cold and constantly hungry. I was at this camp for nearly two and a half years- three and a half overall as a prisoner.

Some of us were sent to Rokuroshi Prison. That was far worse. Again there was very little food- horrible stuff. Our soup was hot water with weeds and plants from the mountains around us. The rice portion was less. Sometimes there were horse bones covered with maggots in the soup. We found snakes and roasted them, and we even ate the larvae from wasps' nests. We were on an agricultural project here. The compound was surrounded with a barbed wire fence. When some of our POW's escaped, they were brought back again and severely punished.

I met a lot of fellows during the war who didn't make it. All in all, I believe there were about 43 Brainerd men who never got back home. Many of them were young, unmarried fellows who said, 'It isn't worth living, Russ.' And in a short time they were dead. From my own experiences, I believe that any person *can will himself to die.* We must have a physical determination to live. I had someone at home depending on me, a wife and children, so I determined to live."

As told to Maxine Russell on April 6, 1988. Russell Swearingen, First Lieutenant US Army retired, and his wife, Eleanore Palmer Swearingen, live in Crow Wing County at Deerwood, Minnesota. They have four children, Donald, Arlene, Danny and Karen and many grandchildren and great-grandchildren.

81

Japanese guard with samurai sword beheading American soldier.

The long Death March. Our forces were weakened by starvation, malaria, dysentery and the hot sun. Note the soldiers to the right front shouldering an exhausted buddy. April 10 - 16, 1942.

BATAAN REMEMBERED:
An Interview with Walter Straka

These are the words of another Bataan Veteran Hero, Walter Straka, an extremely tall and obviously once handsome man, interviewed, April 18, 1988.

"I was born in Brainerd, Minnesota, on October 24, 1919. When I was just out of school, I joined the Minnesota National Guards. I came from a big family of ten children. My father, Frank Straka, was of Czech descent; my mother Mary Sotter Straka, was Austrian. My brother Joe also fought in the war in New Guinea.

When I first arrived with my outfit in the Philippines and saw those big islands full of rivers, mountains and jungles, I thought 'How in Hell will I ever get home!' But I knew we had a job to do, and I was just 21 and strong and ready to do it. It was not long afterwards that our 194th Tank Battalion was in the midst of the war. When all our planes were knocked out at Clark Field and our supply ships destroyed at Pearl Harbor, the Japanese bombers and troops kept increasing steadily. Our chances became less and less when the Japanese crack troops arrived from Singapore. We were almost without ammunition, food and medicine- no quinine and weak from malaria. As a kid, I'd only seen squirrels dying, and how they tremble when stunned. It'll never leave me- seeing so many guys killed and dying!

Finally, on Black Thursday, April 9th, almost exactly 4 months after Pearl Harbor, we realized we were close to defeat. Thank God for General King! If it hadn't been for this very compassionate man, our troops would never have surrendered. We would have gone on fighting to the death. I would have been a dead man.

Then, we were herded together and forced into a Death March. I saw the Jap soldiers bayoneting our men if they stepped out of line for water. I saw them lop off heads with their samurai swords if they tried to leave the line. Our captors were cruel and arrogant. To this day I can feel the place in my back where one of them hit me with his rifle butt when I tried to stoop for water. And there were dead bodies laying all over polluting the water. I was in terrible pain from dehydration. Yes, to this day I sometimes shiver and shake like an injured squirrel.

There were five of us Brainerd buddies who started out on the Death March together. They were Jim McComas, Sid Snign,

83

Ken Porwall, Byron Viellette and myself. We tried to look out for each other. Bryon was the only one of our five to die overseas. He was a great physical specimen of a man, but he came down a short while later with a fatal cerebral malaria. It seemed sometimes the biggest fell first. And then there was Jim McComas, once 213 pounds, who began to drop behind. We shouldered him and walked him along. Anyone who dropped out died. They were bayoneted to death. The Chaplain helped us too. He gave us some hope by saying 'just keep going and you'll be all right.' And Jim made it. All the time maybe ten days that we were on the Death March, we were only fed twice by the Japanese and that was just plain rice. We were penned up in that terrible heat at San Fernando for three days, so it took us longer.

Camp O'Donnell was a filthy rotten place beyond comprehension. Flies were thick- solid on everything. I'll never forget that zigzagging line of thousands of prisoners as far as I could see. Then, I was taken back to Bataan on a truck trip for about 6 or 7 days. We stopped overnight at a school house. Filthy water and we had no blankets. Five days later I came down with Malaria. It was awful- the sweat and freeze- sweat and freeze. By now I'd had just about everything, dysentery, beri-beri, hook worm. Everybody was sick with something. I thought that the most merciful, humane thing would have been to line us all up and kill us instead of starving us to death, but they seemed to enjoy seeing us tortured.

I remember one time when we first reached Camp O'Donnell that a Japanese major addressed us and through his interpreter said, 'We hate the Americans. You're going to die as our prisoners. You'll work the rest of your life for us. The war will last a hundred years!'

Sometimes prisoners were thought dead and so they were put outside the hospital overnight. You see no one could find their heartbeat. But at least one of those fellows that I knew was alive, and he's still alive today. His name is "Chief" and he lives in New Mexico. I often wonder how many of those prisoners were buried alive. There were so many dead bodies. I can still feel stepping on one dead fellow's arm. The slimy meat came off on my shoe and I could see the bones.

At Camp Cabanatuan where we were sent after Camp O'Donnell, I saw one of my fellow prisoners tied hand and foot in the guard post. They wanted all of us to see this as an example.

Each time all day long that our captors came to relieve the guards, they kicked the prisoner in the face with their hobnailed boots- nothing left of his face and his tongue hung out. At night the fellow was dead. He bled to death.

Sometimes a Belgium bishop from Manila came to Camp Cabanatuan. I believe he was the only white visitor we ever had. He would come in his bus with food for us and sometimes messages from Filipino wives. Well, one of our American prisoners had a Filipino wife who wrote him a message to tell him about the kids. She had the note hidden in a coconut. The Japanese happened to break open the coconut and found the message. Then they shot the bishop and burned his bus.

After some months went by, we were taken to a Japanese ship at Manila by way of Camp Bilibid. I remember we were loaded at noon. Hundreds of men were stacked on top of each other in the hold. I just lay there prone, almost suffocated to death. We were so packed we couldn't sit down. Every day they'd drop a pail of rice down the hatch and some of the foulest water. We were like hungry dogs going after those rice balls. Humans can get just like animals.

When night came on, there was only a tiny ten watt light bulb burning. We could barely see. Finally a guy let me put my head on his leg. When I awoke, here was someone I knew from Brainerd, John Falconer. Everybody was sick with dysentery- so weak they couldn't get up the ladder. We had to let it go everywhere- all over the floor. The pails couldn't hold it. It was horrible, the filth, the smell and the suffocation. Later I heard that one demented prisoner slit a fellow's throat and sucked his blood. On that Hell Ship there were more insane than sane. Hundreds of prisoners died and were thrown into the sea. We were traveling in a convoy, but none of our ships were marked Hospital Ships. Our subs didn't know that there were POW's on those ships so we lost a lot of our men in those convoys.

In Japan I was taken to Fukuoka Number Three to work in the steel mill. My weight had dropped from 194 pounds when I first went overseas to 89 pounds. I was all skin and bones.

The morning that the second A Bomb was scheduled for the Kukura area, I was up on the third story of the steel mill mixing chemicals for the open hearth furnace. I heard the Japanese air raid sirens. Everyone took off, but I figured it was fruitless for me to run that distance for the tunnels. That morning fortunately we were heavily clouded in so the bomb never fell on us.

85

It fell on Nagasaki. I always say that if it hadn't been for a cloud in the sky, I wouldn't be here. My life's been like a spider's thread. Fragile. One little mistake and I would have been dead. So many times I've experienced this strange feeling. It was by the Grace of God that I didn't get killed. Many others right around me died or got killed.

After the A Bomb was dropped on nearby Nagasaki, some of us were put on a work force for about 18 hours to help clean up the ruins. The Japanese couldn't have known that the fallout was dangerous. When they realized that the ground was contaminated, they moved everybody out of the area. For about eight years after the war was over and I was back in the States, I had to give monthly blood samples, but they couldn't find any damage. However, some others who worked around me died later of Leukemia.

I guess I was lucky to make it back home after three and a half years of torture, imprisonment, hunger, disease and loneliness. Afterwards, I visited the parents of some of my dead buddies who lived here in Brainerd. If I had told these parents the truth about their sons' deaths, they would have died broken-hearted."

Walter B. Straka, Corporal US Army retired, was married in 1946 to Cleta Sylvester. They have seven children, Marcia, Gregory, Paul, Elizabeth, Jane, Peter and Sarah and seven grandchildren.

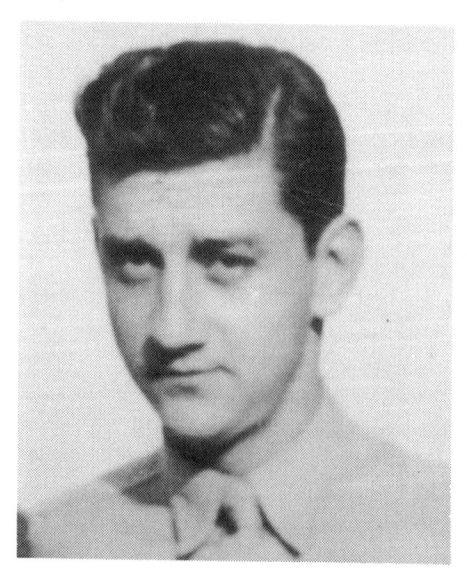

Before: July 1941, taken at Brainerd, MN.

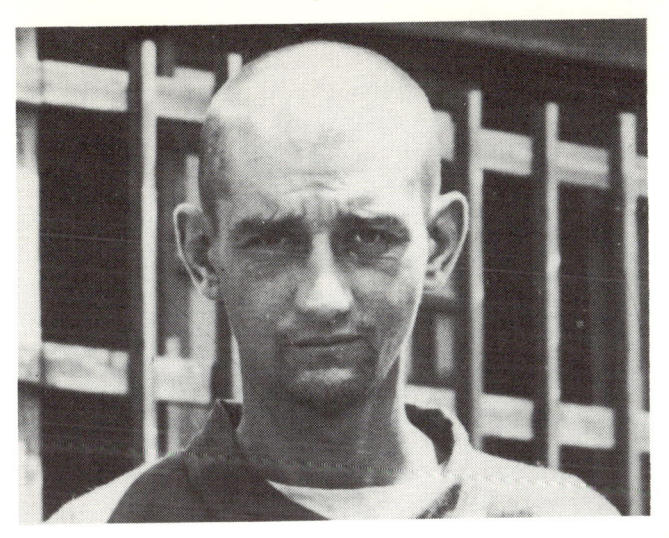

After: 1944, in Japanese Prison Camp Fukuoka #3. I was #1130, all my hair was gone from malaria.

BATAAN REMEMBERED:
As told by Henry Peck

On the evening of April 25, 1988, the interviewer, Maxine Russell, was invited to the home of Henry and Erma Peck on North Long Lake to hear this most harrowing and heroic story. Henry Peck, a trim man with a kind smile, in his late sixties, is a survivor of the Bataan Death March. He is one of only three survivors from Company "A" 194th Tank Battalion, currently living in Crow Wing County. Here's his frightening story:

I was born on New Year's Day, January 1, 1921, in Beetle County, Huron, South Dakota, of Scotch-Irish ancestry. We were a family of 4 boys and 3 girls, all raised on a farm. Both my grandparents had it rough. My parents didn't have it easy either, so I guess I'm tough because of it. I'm glad I wasn't born into an easy life. It fitted me for what was to follow. In 1940 I was nineteen years old, and I knew I would soon be drafted. Then I heard of Company "A" Tank Battalion at Brainerd and signed up. We were trained out at Fort Lewis, Washington. It was here I met Dr. Leo Schneider of Portland, Oregon. He stayed with the First Detail and went along with us all the way. I admired him.

87

When I got to Manila, I thought I'd never seen a dirtier city in all my life. It was like a barnyard. I remember seeing poor people everywhere earning about 50 cents a day. I noticed quite a few two-wheeled buggies drawn by small calesa ponies for transportation. The traffic was an awful jumble with people and buses going all directions. I wanted to turn right around and go back to Brainerd.

I was in Reconnaissance. We were watching for parachute troops. The Japanese flew in over the Clark Field area with 54 bombers. We counted them. I caught the first three bombings. I was close by. A week or so after the destruction of Clark Field and Nichols Field, I was sent to Fort Stotsenburg again. We were loading ammo. At the second air raid, I took to the ditch. Afterwards, we pulled out in a hurry- even left our foot lockers. We couldn't figure out why MacArthur didn't get us to retaliate. Why? Didn't we have any more bombers?

Well, we moved out and below Manila. Some of us in Reconnaissance were watching and waiting for the Japanese troops to land in SE Luzon, and some at Lingayen Gulf. Then, one Company "C" went South and Company "A" went North. From up there, the 192nd and 194th Battalions gradually pulled to the South.

I was in a half-track. A half-track looked like a truck but it

Pfc. Henry Peck with a training tank at Fort Lewis, Wa.

had tank tracks behind it. I'll never forget that Christmas Eve-1941. We came up on our rear echelon. I remember Jim McComas and Lt. Costigan were there. Colonel Ernest Miller was setting up a road block at Carmen on the Agno River. Colonel Miller wanted another half-track to block the road. I volunteered. So did my buddy Alberg. (He is now living in Sand Point, Idaho.) That's the way we stopped three Japanese tanks. Our forces had to get through to protect a Filipino train carrying two train loads of our Filipino Army. We got there in time, and the train went through. This was in open rice paddy country. It was night. We were looking around for ground troops. The Japs fired at us, but I gave a blast back with my 50 caliber machine gun. There was no response from the enemy. It was real dark, and all was quiet after that. Our tank battalions held the line. On the Agno River, we had 30 tanks and 5 halftracks, and we held a 25 mile defense line. We covered the withdrawal of our troops to Bataan. We slowed down the Japanese advances. Actually, we were very important to our Army and our Country at that time.

Then, we moved to Angeles for a week. We didn't know where our tanks were. We couldn't get them across the river because the bridge was blown out. On New Year's Eve, we pulled back into Bataan. Now we were soon cut down to two meals a day. We knew we were outnumbered. From the beginning, the Japanese Army had 100,000 troops- some were crack troops which had fought in China. And our Army had a great many "green" troops. Much later on, I ran into some Japanese engineers who also had fought in China. They seemed to respect us as soldiers. We thought, because Japan was such a small country, it was quite an accomplishment for them to conquer our troops. I wonder what was wrong with our officers? In Hawaii they had warnings. Why didn't they send our B17 and B18 bombers to help us? 'Hold on, they'd say! Help's on the way!' Sure it was, but *42 months* later!'

Well, we got less and less food. I was on the east side of Bataan. I didn't have any injuries, but I had malaria and dysentery bad. I was given charcoal to help me for dysentery. The water was lousy and mosquitoes everywhere! I had dry Beri-beri too. My feet and legs were all swollen.

I started on the Death March somewhat above Mariveles. It was a four day march for me. I was weak, terribly hot and thirsty. The Japanese soldiers wouldn't let us fill our canteens as we passed the artesian wells. They wanted to torture us. One night we stayed inside an old sugar mill. All we got to eat on the entire trip was one rice ball the size of a tea cup. I saw 4 or 5 fellows bayoneted to death when they dropped out of line. It was unbelievably cruel. One of our soldiers jumped to his death off a bridge and into an old river bed. One fellow named Julius Knudsen had something wrong with his hip. Later, I saw him riding on a truck. He waved to me, but that was the last time I ever saw him. The Japs generally killed those who couldn't walk.

They even shot their own men. They didn't value life. I remember one Japanese soldier who had been drinking. He was really intoxicated. Two other Japs helped hold him up as they walked along. Well, I watched the Japanese officer take this man, one of his own men, into the bamboo, and there he shot him. Bamboo made a good cover. It grew thick and tall.

First, I was at Camp O'Donnell, the Death Camp. It was a shocking experience. I watched helplessly as hundreds and hundreds of prisoners died right around me. There were flies around everywhere on the sick, the dying; most of them dying from thirst and starvation. Finally, after some weeks, we were

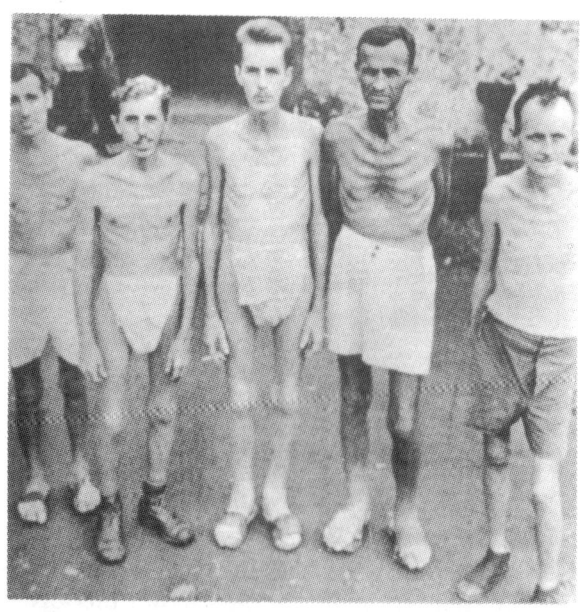

Liberated US Prisoners, starvation at Bilibid Prison, Manila.

moved to Camp Cabanatuan. I was terribly weak and hungry. One day five of our prisoners escaped through the fence. Well, they caught them and shot them right in front of us.

With a number of other prisoners, I was moved in Dec. 1942 from Cabanatuan to Lipa-Bantanga. Here it was all rough labor- pick and shovel and wheelbarrow. We were here to build a big air runway about a mile and a half long. I remember there were 370 American and 1,000 Filipino prisoners. But we got three quite good meals a day, mostly horsemeat, carabao and some fish. If you broke out of prison, there was always some Filipino who would sell you back to the Japanese for 50 dollars. Once when some prisoners ran away, the Japanese guards blamed it on the cooks. Then, they tied those cooks out in the hot sun and put broom handles under their knees. They couldn't walk after that. You bet they were cruel!

In March of 1944, we were moved to Camp Murray, a Philippine airbase. We were put to work knocking the dikes from off the rice beds to make more runways. Then, we reworked the ground with lava rock covered with dirt. But we had a few schemes of our own. Here's where we flipped over 17 Japanese fighter planes. What we did was not completely fill in all the holes in the ground. When the planes speeded for take-off, they sunk in the soft ground and flipped forward. That knocked them out of commission so we had a little revenge.

When our American planes began to hit there in September 1944,we were moved to Bilibid Prison, Manila. More starvation. Each day we only received half of a canteen cup, about a pint of cornmeal mush. At Bilibid I met some old friends again, Dr. Schneider, our Tank doctor and another doctor I knew from the Nichols Field Detail. Also, Lt. Carrol Guin, Captain Arthur Root and Walt Samuelson, all from Company "A" were there. We were all supposed to leave for Japan on the same ship, an old French freighter, one that hauled coal. It was so crowded that us prisoners were standing around on the coal. I don't know if these fellows were in our convoy, but I do know that all three of them never made it to Japan.

At first there were 11 ships in our convoy. We called our ship the "Banjo" Maru. The conditions were unbelievably filthy. We were only allowed one canteen of water a day, and we were fed very little "Lugow"- a watery rice. It was so hot in the hold that many men went completely crazy. Some killed others and actually sucked their blood. Every morning there were many another death. But the men I worked with in the work camps stuck together as best we could.

We were 39 days getting to Japan. The 3rd and 4th day out, we ran into a submarine blockade. Our boat got through the blockade. Only three boats out of eleven got through. We were in the bay at Hong Kong for ten days. Then the Americans bombed us. Now, the Japs took us East towards Formosa. The day that they told us they were taking us off the boat, an American Reconnaissance plane flew over us. We were scared to death when they took us back out to sea, but then they brought us back again. Oh, yes, every time when the torpedos were dropped close by, they covered our hatch with tarpaulins so that the water wouldn't seep into the hold. While at Formosa, we were transferred from the "Banjo" maru, our Hell Ship, into a Japanese Troop Transport. It was great. We weren't cramped, and we had three good meals a day and blankets. We couldn't believe it. Why suddenly such good treatment?

Finally, we arrived in Japan. Some of us were taken to "Shako" (Kosaka) in the NW corner of Japan where it was very cold. Dr. Schneider who stayed with the First Detail went to the coal mines. Here at "Shako" we wore Japanese clothes, a huge blouse, World War I pants and Japanese tennis shoes that were very cold when wet. It seemed I was always cold and hungry. We were mostly served rice, sometimes meat, seaweed, very long radishes (about a foot long) and roasted grasshoppers. I never expected to eat South Dakota grasshoppers from the state where I was born. The Japanese had years previously brought these in from North and South Dakota and roasted them. The protein was probably good for us. I remember once watching some women in the Philippines picking Junebugs which they ate for their protein too. And we had lots of blue lice, about the size of a matchhead, but nobody tried to eat them! They bit me around the waist until my skin was just like raw hamburger. I couldn't seem to get rid of those lice.

I was a prisoner in a hilly part of Japan. I worked in a copper smelter. I didn't find the work too hard. We were on 8 hour shifts, sometimes 16 hour shifts. We worked alongside Japanese civilians, probably men from the Korean Work Detail. The barracks though were unheated, an A-roofed deal. There was no wood to burn and *it was cold!* We had a straw mat to sleep on, and a blanket and comforter. The Japanese took us to work and brought us back again, and they finally gave us enough water.

One of the guards would bring us rice in bags made of straw.

I asked him if we could shake the leavings out of the bags for a little extra food. Three weeks before the surrender, he stopped giving us the rice bag leavings and began eating them himself. That made us wonder how the war was going?

At the time of the surrender, I was on a 11 to 7 night shift. One of the prisoners, a Mexican, who came down to relieve us said we should be up at the barracks by ten o'clock. We had so many rumors of peace before that I didn't believe him. After breakfast, I had just fallen asleep when I heard a big commotion. The Detail came back shouting, "The War is over!" I couldn't believe it yet. At one o'clock we were called to the compound. Our Japanese Camp Commander told us that Japan and America "have shook hands." It was August 15, 1945. A strange feeling came over me, like a good dream hard to believe.

I was at "Shako" for another month until they started us home. We were detoured to a Red Cross boat, deloused and given new clothes. Then we were taken to Tokyo. The evening of September 16, we came into Yokohama Bay. Here we were put on a large US ship, given steaks and the best meal I'd had in almost four years. At night we slept in hammocks. Next we flew from Tokyo to Okinawa. The following day, after we left our "Kitchen," there was a tremendous typhoon that completely flattened the kitchen, and even turned over ships. It was another narrow escape for me. Just lucky, I guess.

And now for another two weeks, we were taken back to Manila again- Manila, the city where in 1941 it all began! We were trucked to an Army Transport, and sixteen days later, we arrived in San Francisco. Here at the Presidio, I saw an Army doctor for the first time. From there I was sent to Schick General Hospital in Clinton, Iowa. First I was given a nine-day furlough and again a thirty-day furlough at Christmas and New Year. At Camp McCoy, Wisconsin, I was given an even longer ninety-day furlough again. I suppose because of our long imprisonment, about 3 1/2 years, a slow discharge was thought best. At last in May 1946, I was discharged at Fort Sheridan near Chicago, Illinois.

I was lucky too that my folks were still alive and well when I got home. It felt wonderful to be back, but I also felt very sad for the families of my many friends in Company "A" who didn't make it.

Corporal Henry Peck was married October 19, 1946 to Lilah Sinclair who died on January 18, 1987. He married Erma Hollingsworth on November 21, 1987. There are ten children and fifteen grandchildren.

Six American Officers, Prisoners at Zentsuji Prison Camp, from left to right, Col. E. B. Miller, Major Scotty Muir, Major L. E. Johnson, Major Edward Burke, Lt. John Hummel and Lt. Russell Swearingen. Spring 1945. A Japanese Photo

A new M26 - General Pershing Tank. Eight Brainerd veterans pictured above are Capt. James L. Johnson, standing, Intelligence officer for the 194th; middle row, left to right, K. J. Porwoll and James McComas; upper right, left to right, Lee MacDonald, William Mattson, Walt Straka, Pete Clabo and Russell Swearingen. Minneapolis Tribune 1940

Colonel Ernest B. Miller, Commander of the 194th Tank Battalion (Minnesota National Guard) and World War II hero at Bataan, was the recipient of the Medal of Valor, Minnesota's highest military decoration "for exceptional gallantry and intrepidity." He was also author of **Bataan Uncensored.** Colonel Miller died in February 1959. He was survived by his wife, Anne, and his daughters Marilyn and Patricia, and sons Thomas and Richard. Their eldest son, James, was killed at Anzio, Italy.

Photo Minneapolis Tribune, Jan. 25, 1948

On September 7, 1986, fifty Bataan veterans were honored at Brainerd, Minnesota, when decorated with bronze star medals for valorous conduct in the defense of the Philippines. Officers with the 1st Squadron, 194th Cavalry of the Minnesota Army National Guard released the following list at the ceremony:

James Bogart, Henry Peck, Kenneth Porwoll, Clifford Rardin, Walter B. Straka, Russell Swearingen, Ralph Hollingsworth, Hortense McKay, Anton Cichy, Bernard Fitzpatrick, Harold Kurvers, William McKeon, Phillip Tripp, Harold Van Alstyne, Ronal Weber, Robert Boyer, Ken Davis, Anton Urban, Ray Makepiece.

Mel Ahlgrim, August Bender, Alpheus Brown, Billie E. Brown, Ernest M. Gordon, Kenneth Gordon, Carrol Guin, Eugene T. Noglund, David E. Karlson, Wesley J. Kerigan, Julius Knudsen, Howard Larson, Lee MacDonald, Roy Maghan, James F. McComas, Ernest B. Miller, Donald H. Paine, Walter H. Samuelson, Herbert Strobel.

Boyce Hyatt, Robert Swanson, Edward Burke, William J. Smith, Gerald J. Bell, Arthur Root, John Falconer and Roy Nordstrom.

———— *May we ever be mindful of their valor!*

MEMORIAL BATAAN DEATH MARCH COMPANY "A" 194TH TANK BATTALION *located at the Brainerd Armory, SE corner 5th & Laurel Streets. Mrs. Lee MacDonald, left, and Mrs. Jim McComas, right, stand beside this memorial erected summer 1972 to honor their husbands and all the 77 members of the Bataan Death March.* Brainerd Daily Dispatch

    Through the years there have existed many deep bonds of friendship between the wives, widows and children of these men. The families at home suffered immeasurable anguish and heartbreak. One of the women spoke of her terror every time the phone rang. Brainerd was the hardest hit of any city of its size by the fall of Bataan.

Epilogue

The Brainerd area is distinguished in that, in World War II, it had a heroine of mercy in the Philippines, Hortense McKay, and a combat hero, Ernie Miller, whose men of the 194th Tank Battalion had an important role in meeting the invading Japanese forces and then enduring the Death March, Hell ships and prison camps.

When American victory was ultimately achieved, the common cause of these friends and neighbors of ours in the conflict to uphold American ideals is vividly described by Ernie Miller when he told of the scene at Camp Rokuroshi, in Japan when upon the Japanese surrender, the American prisoners took command of the prison. He said in his book, Bataan Uncensored: "The flagpole was a scrawny thing, but the best we could find. It was soon to hold the symbol of free men. Old Glory, in all her beauty and majesty was slowly raised as an American sounded 'To the Colors' on a Japanese bugle. The Japanese commandant and the guards stood at rigid attention. They saluted as the flag went skyward, her folds spreading out to silently greet the clear skies up above and to gesture a token that all was well to the upturned prisoners' faces, below. Among those faces, there were few dry eyes. I thought of words that had been stamped indelibly on my memory during those years of prison life - words of Old Glory, could she but speak. She would say 'I swing before your eyes a bright gleam of color, a symbol of yourself. My stars and stripes are your dreams and your labors. They are bright with courage, firm with faith, because you have made them so, out of your hearts. For you are the makers of me, your flag, and it is well that you glory in the making'."

Being well acquainted with both Hortense McKay and Ernie Miller and knowing Russell Swearingen, Walter Straka, Henry Peck and many of the men mentioned by them, I can attest that our flag is truly a symbol of themselves, their dreams, their labors, their courage, and their hearts born out of a steadfast faith in and love for their country.

Having made two combat landings in the retaking of the Philippines and while serving in General MacArthur's headquarters, I had the opportunity to retrace the death march, visit Corregidor and learn more of the heroic role of the 194th Tank Battalion. Therefore, when Ernie Miller asked me to reorganize the battalion, I deemed it an honor to undertake the task.

The new 194th Tank Battalion was reorganized in late 1946

and early 1947 with units in Princeton, Milaca, Aitkin, Crosby, Brainerd and Long Prairie. It was ordered to active duty in the Korean War with many of our men engaging in combat in Korea.

At the end of the Korean conflict, the battalion was again reorganized and the Brainerd unit is now called Headquarters and Headquarters Troop, 1st Squadron, 194th Cavalry with a detached unit in Milaca and in Iowa and with Troop A in Grand Rapids and Aitkin and Troops B, C and D in Iowa. Although called cavalry, the squadron is equipped with tanks. Having retained the numerical designation of 194th, the heritage persists and is cause for a fine esprit which should never cease. The history of the 194th Tank Battalion shows the importance of the National Guard citizen soldier who sacrifices for his country in time of need and then goes about his civilian pursuits maintaining a posture of preparedness.

And we will always need women like Hortense McKay!

Carl E. Erickson

Carl E. Erickson, Lt. Col. U. S. Army retired, resides with his wife, Eunice, at 323 North Seventh Street, Brainerd, Minnesota. He is the senior partner in the law firm of Erickson, Casey, Erickson and Charpentier. He has had a distinguished career in his profession and in other civilian pursuits and he served in various capacities in World War II including that of Acting Chief of the Military Government Section in General MacArthur's Headquarters. He reorganized and took the new 194th Tank Battalion to duty in the Korean War. He has been awarded the decorations of Legion of Merit, Bronze Star Medal, Philippine Commonwealth Medal of Merit and the State of Minnesota Medal of Merit.

On Memorial Day, Monday, May 30, 1988, Lt. Col. Carl E. Erickson, was the principal speaker at the Ground Breaking Ceremony for the new Brainerd National Guard Armory at Brainerd Industrial Park. The new building is designed to house the 150 man troop, Squadron Headquarters. The size of the Armory will be 37,211 square feet at a cost of $2,051,612. The unit strength will be 122 personnel to include 16 fulltime soldiers.

After the Presentation of Colors by 1-194th Cavalry, American Legion, Veterans of Foreign Wars and the Marine Corps League, the Brainerd High School Band played the National Anthem. Distinguished guests who appeared on the program were: Captain Cliff Olson, Chaplain Major Steven Schaitberger, Major Dan Holmes, Mayor James Brown, Mary Koep, Chairperson Crow Wing County Commissioners, Brigadier General John Cox, State Representatives Paul Theide and Steve Wenzel, and the first Commander of the reorganized 194th after WWII, Carl E. Erickson.

PREPAREDNESS

IS AN IMPORTANT

INSTRUMENT

OF LIBERTY AND PEACE.

Photo Album

Part I

Introduction
1. Among the wildflowers on the family farm near Harmony, Minnesota.
2. Two little girls with bows in their hair.
3. George McKay family at Gull Lake.
4. Hortense as a student nurse in uniform.

Destination: The Philippines
5. US Army Transport Grant.
6. 2nd Lt. Hortense McKay arrives at Fort Stotsenburg.
7. Hortense McKay and Jessie Locke, Manila.
8. Malinta Tunnel entrance.
9. Lateral of Malinta Tunnel Hospital.

Bataan Jungle
10. Bathing in the Real River at Hospital #2, Bataan.
11. Outdoor hospital #2.
12. Maps of Bataan Peninsula and "The Rock"

The Valiant Men of the USS Spearfish
13. Rescued by submarine, the USS Spearfish.

Conclusion
14. Hortense McKay, University of Minnesota, 1949.
15. McKay receives her certificate of retirement.
16. At Naval District Headquarters.
17. Three hundred foot cross.
18. Tablet to the Angels of Bataan and Corregidor.
19. McKay receives her bronze star medal.
20. McKay is buried in Scotland Churchyard Cemetery.

Part II

Bataan Remembered
21. 80 members of Company "A".
22. Battle of Bataan
23. Sergeant Herbert Strobel.
24. Bataan Death March.
25. Brainerd soldiers on the Bataan Death March.
26. Another view of Death March.
27. A Japanese guard beheading one of our soldiers.
28. The long Bataan Death March weakened by starvation, malaria, dysentery and hot sun.
29. Walter Straka.
30. Walter Straka afterwards as a prisoner.
31. Pfc. Henry Peck.
32. Starvation at Bilibid Prison.
33. Six American officers of Company "A" prisoners at Zentsuji.
34. A new M26- General Pershing - Tank, with 8 Brainerd veterans.
35. Colonel Ernest B. Miller, Commander 194th Tank Battalion.
36. Memorial erected in 1972 at Brainerd, Minnesota.

BATAAN MEMORIAL

Groundbreaking — Brainerd Armory, 1988
Photo by Maxine Russell

"What a new face courage puts on everything!"

Ralph Waldo Emerson
Letters and Social Aims:
Resources

Part II

Bataan Remembered
21. 80 members of Company "A".
22. Battle of Bataan
23. Sergeant Herbert Strobel.
24. Bataan Death March.
25. Brainerd soldiers on the Bataan Death March.
26. Another view of Death March.
27. A Japanese guard beheading one of our soldiers.
28. The long Bataan Death March weakened by starvation, malaria, dysentery and hot sun.
29. Walter Straka.
30. Walter Straka afterwards as a prisoner.
31. Pfc. Henry Peck.
32. Starvation at Bilibid Prison.
33. Six American officers of Company "A" prisoners at Zentsuji.
34. A new M26- General Pershing - Tank, with 8 Brainerd veterans.
35. Colonel Ernest B. Miller, Commander 194th Tank Battalion.
36. Memorial erected in 1972 at Brainerd, Minnesota.

BATAAN MEMORIAL

Groundbreaking — Brainerd Armory, 1988
Photo by Maxine Russell

"*What a new face courage puts on everything!*"

Ralph Waldo Emerson
Letters and Social Aims:
Resources